Taking Minutes of Meetings

Taking Minutes of Meetings

Joanna Gutmann | Revised Second Edition

KoganPage

LONDON PHILADELPHIA N

Publisher's note
Every possible effort has been made to ensure that the information contained in this book is accurate at the time of going to press, and the publishers and authors cannot accept responsibility for any errors or omissions, however caused. No responsibility for loss or damage occasioned to any person acting, or refraining from action, as a result of the material in this publication can be accepted by the editor, the publisher or the author.

First published in 2001
Second edition 2006
Revised second edition 2010

Apart from any fair dealing for the purposes of research or private study, or criticism or review, as permitted under the Copyright, Designs and Patents Act 1988, this publication may only be reproduced, stored or transmitted, in any form or by any means, with the prior permission in writing of the publishers, or in the case of reprographic reproduction in accordance with the terms and licences issued by the CLA. Enquiries concerning reproduction outside these terms should be sent to the publishers at the undermentioned addresses:

120 Pentonville Road	525 South 4th Street, #241	4737/23 Ansari Road
London N1 9JN	Philadelphia PA 19147	Daryaganj
United Kingdom	USA	New Delhi 110002
www.koganpage.com		India

© Joanna Gutmann, 2001, 2006, 2010

The right of Joanna Gutmann to be identified as the author of this work has been asserted by her in accordance with the Copyright, Designs and Patents Act 1988.

ISBN 978 0 7494 6029 7
E-ISBN 978 0 7494 5892 8

British Library Cataloguing-in-Publication Data

A CIP record for this book is available from the British Library.

Library of Congress Cataloging-in-Publication Data

Gutmann, Joanna.
 Taking minutes of meetings / Joanna Gutmann. -- Rev. 2nd ed.
 p. cm.
 Includes bibliographic references.
 ISBN 978-0-7494-5657-3
 1. Business meetings. 2. Business communication. 3. Corporate minutes. 4. Business records. I Title.
 HF5734.5.G88 2010
 658.4'56--dc22

 2009035457

Typeset by Jean Cussons Typesetting, Diss, Norfolk
Printed and bound in India by Replika Press Pvt Ltd

Contents

Introduction

Minutes are vital to the success of the meeting. Participants rely on them for information on subjects they did not understand or to fill in gaps when they lost concentration. The action points act as a reminder to those who agreed in the heat of the moment but have since been overtaken by other priorities and would otherwise forget what they were to do. Those who could not attend need an idea of what was decided in their absence. And finally, minutes are the historical record of the meeting and 'proof' of the actions/outcomes.

For a role that carries significant responsibility, there is very little support for the minute-taker. There is a common misconception that secretaries can take minutes. This seems to stem from two sources: first, the word 'secretary' as in committee secretary; secondly, the idea that taking minutes is about speed and secretaries can write fast, particularly if they have shorthand.

In fact, a secretary is only a little more likely to be trained to take minutes than to be a company secretary. The perception that minute taking is all about speed is also wrong. Ask secretaries what they are typing and they are likely to have to look at it before

answering – typing does not involve the brain on a conscious level; shorthand is similarly a mechanical skill, and so is scribbling the words that someone says.

The key skill for taking minutes is the ability to listen to the words someone is saying, absorb them, evaluate the manner of the delivery and identify the speaker's point of view – the message. It is ongoing listening and simultaneous summarising. Although a good shorthand writer can take down the words and summarise them back in the office, it is a long drawn-out process and few can afford the time.

Assuming that the minute-taker gets involved in the setting up of the meeting, as many do, there is also the need for good administration skills, particularly in today's world where meetings are often rescheduled, rooms are in short supply, budgets are being cut and time is at a premium for all concerned.

There is a second type of minute-taker: people who attend to contribute but find themselves taking the notes in the absence of an available secretary. Although they have the advantages of higher status within the group and a better understanding, they also suffer from the problems of identifying what to write. In addition, they may not be trained typists and thus find presenting the minutes in a professional style difficult.

The people who attend my courses have a range of problems with the role, mainly to do with the issue of what to write or coping in a badly led meeting. Quite a few report sleepless nights before a meeting and feelings of stress before, during and after it. Few have received any training, and although many have been taking minutes for years, the lack of clear focus and structure for the meetings has made them wonder about the 'theory' behind the practice.

Today, meetings are far less structured than in the past and it is generally felt that there are many more of them, probably far too many. Very few people believe this to be a good thing; the time taken (and often wasted) by meetings is resented by those who attend as well as by those who minute. Meetings that are

well run are appreciated by everyone, and the minute-taker plays a large part in achieving this. Although it is the chairperson who 'fronts' and controls the meeting, it is the support of the minute-taker that enables this to be done effectively.

In most organisations, there are no 'rules' for minutes: some want formality, others a more casual style; some want all the detail, others only a list of action points. Any guidance is usually limited to house style for layout, not content. The minute-taker has to be flexible and responsive to the needs of both the chairperson and the group.

The minute-taker is one of the most important and powerful people in a meeting. Although the task can be daunting, it is the opportunity to develop your knowledge, broaden your horizons and build your credibility within the organisation. With a clear idea of your role and responsibilities, knowledge of what you are meant to do and some confidence in yourself, your role of minute-taker can even be enjoyable!

Using the book

The book is intended to be used as a reference book. It follows the cycle of a meeting from the decision to hold one through to the dispatch of the minutes. You can read it from cover to cover or dip in to find the help you need on any given aspect of the minute-taker's role.

It is assumed that you have little or no knowledge of the 'theory' of minute taking, although you may have plenty of experience. The book is laid out with lots of headings and with short paragraphs. This will help you to skip the information you already know or don't need for your meetings, and focus on the detail you want.

Terms

A number of terms are used throughout the book as I've tried to

avoid repetition, and these may mean different things to different people. The following explains my meaning:

- *Meeting.* An event involving a group of people, getting together to discuss and/or decide.
- *Committee.* The group of people who are meeting, even though it may not be a formally constituted committee. I've also used the terms group, team, panel, etc.
- *Chairperson.* The person who is leading the meeting. Could also be a facilitator, mediator, convener.
- *Secretary/minute-taker.* The person who is responsible for the administration of the meeting: setting it up, preparing the agenda, dealing with the room booking, coffee, etc, taking the minutes and so on. Although I've used the two titles at random throughout the book, some will argue that a secretary does all the tasks above, while a minute-taker simply takes the minutes, types them up and distributes them. Throughout the book, I've assumed that you are responsible for all aspects of the administration – just ignore the bits that don't apply to your work.

1

Background

Meetings fall into one of two categories – the one-off and the regular. They are generally held to spread information, to discuss issues, to solve problems and/or to decide on future action.

A meeting can be a positive or negative experience, depending on the skill of the chairperson and the attitude of those attending. The most common complaints from those who attend are:

- **Participants couldn't have their say.**
- **Discussion degenerated into argument.**
- **The meeting was dominated by one or two 'loud voices'.**
- **The chairperson took over.**
- **The chairperson did nothing to control the meeting.**
- **Irrelevant discussion was allowed.**
- **It was generally a waste of time (and often stressful through anger and frustration).**

From the minute-taker's point of view, the first of the above complaints is not relevant, but the others are. A meeting that is

badly structured and uncontrolled will definitely be stressful and frustrating and will waste far more time than just the allotted span. The time taken in sorting the notes and typing up the minutes can add hours to the workload.

On the basis that 'time is money', meetings are expensive. Try the exercise in Figure 1.1 for one of your meetings.

Add up the annual salaries of those attending		£	
Add 25% on-cost	+ 25% =	£	
Divide by 52 (weeks of the year)	÷ 52 =	£	
Divide by standard hours per week (eg 37)	÷ 37 =	£	= cost per hour
Multiply by time of meeting (eg 2 hours)	× 2 =	£	
Add in any costs of room hire, refreshments	+ £ =	£	= cost of meeting

Using this calculation, eight people earning £30,000 per annum, meeting for two hours, will cost the organisation around £325. Is it worth it?

Figure 1.1 Calculating the cost of a meeting

There is far more to the meeting than just the time spent around the table. In order to be successful, everybody must:

- **know why they are there;**
- **recognise what is to be achieved;**
- **have read all paperwork in advance;**
- **be prepared (mental and practical preparation);**
- **contribute positively;**
- **listen;**
- **focus and keep to the point;**
- **leave with a clear understanding of any points they should action.**

The minute-taker has a role to play in several of the points above – like so many things, good preparation will make for a good meeting. The agenda should give information as to the purpose of the meeting, the structure it will follow and the preparation that needs to be done. It must be dispatched in time for this to be useful. The minutes will define the action points and serve as a reminder for those who agreed to take responsibility.

Cycle of a meeting

The cycle shown in Figure 1.2 assumes a monthly meeting, held on the 1st of each month. The bracketed number indicates the target date for each action.

For less frequent meetings, the principle of agenda dispatched a week before, minutes despatched within a week should still hold. For weekly meetings, the dates generally change from a week to a couple of days.

For many people, the cycle of the meeting will seem to set impossibly tight deadlines, but:

- **If you do not like typing up your minutes, they only get worse with procrastination.**
- **If you are going to have to ring and ask a participant for guidance on the content, it is better to do it whilst he or she can remember what was said.**
- **If the minutes are not circulated quickly, the action points are a waste of time; it will be too late for participants to take action.**
- **You look inefficient if the minutes are not circulated until the next month's meeting.**

The stages in the cycle

- *First draft of minutes*
 (one day after the meeting)

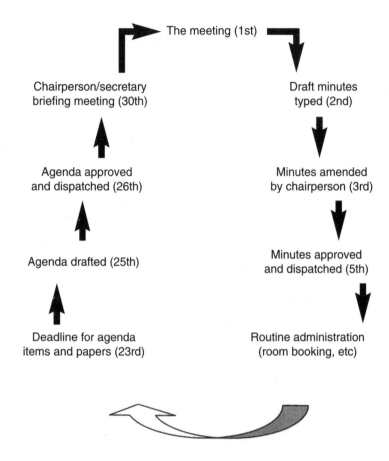

Figure 1.2 Cycle of a meeting

The first draft should be the minutes, typed as the minute-taker perceives the discussion. They may well contain gaps where the chairperson's guidance is needed, but should be as near complete as possible.
- *Chairperson's approval*
(two to three days after meeting)
The chairperson should check the minutes for factual

accuracy and 'political correctness' – phrasing that may cause offence or that does not represent the view of the group. The chairperson should not add any extra information or change the minutes to suit personal views.

- *Minutes dispatched*
 (five days after meeting)
 The minutes should be sent to all committee members and anyone else who gets a copy. Any papers that were distributed at the meeting should be attached for those who did not attend.
- *Routine administration*
 The booking of rooms, coffee, etc usually falls to the minute-taker. Throughout the book you'll find advice and guidance on improving the meeting's effectiveness through these routine tasks.
- *Deadline for agenda items*
 (around eight days before next meeting)
 Under 'Date of next meeting' in the minutes, a deadline for agenda items should have been given (see Chapter 11). Anything that is received after this can be dealt with under 'Any other business'. All papers for discussion at the meeting must be submitted by this date so they can be included with the agenda. In reality, the secretary is usually left to ring or e-mail to nag participants for agenda items and papers.
- *Draft agenda*
 (seven days before next meeting)
 The secretary should put together the agenda and pass it to the chairperson for approval.
- *Agenda dispatched*
 (one week before next meeting)
 Each participant should receive an agenda and all papers that are to be discussed. The agenda should be cross-referenced to indicate which papers relate to each agenda item. Hints as to other preparation may be included (see Chapter 4).

- *Briefing*
 (one to two days before next meeting)
 The chairperson and minute-taker should meet to
 discuss the content of the meeting, identify any
 problem areas and deal with any concerns either party
 has about the meeting. This is seldom a formal event,
 but is often a brief chat before, or on the way to, the
 meeting. The formality will be influenced by the style of
 the people involved and the importance of the meeting.
- *The meeting*
 If the rest of the cycle of the meeting is in place, the
 event itself should be efficient and successful.

The participants

There are four roles in a meeting: to lead it (chairperson), to
support it (secretary), to contribute to it or to observe it. Only one
person can take each of the first two roles, but they are closely
interlinked – the management of the meeting shared by two
people. Any number can attend or observe.

The participants are responsible for a certain amount of work
before, during and after the meeting.

The chairperson

Before the meeting:

- Decide that the meeting is necessary.
- Identify participants (who needs to attend all/just part
 of the meeting).
- Approve the agenda.
- Brief the minute-taker.
- Prepare self (content, participants, where actions are
 necessary).

During the meeting:

- Introduce newcomers and visitors.
- Inform the delegates of the agreed behaviours (eg how decisions will be reached).
- Control the agenda (discussion time and order).
- Control delegate contributions.
- Work with and support the minute-taker.

After the meeting:

- Approve the minutes within three days of the meeting.
- Collect and assess any feedback.
- Support participants with their action points where necessary.

The minute-taker

Before the meeting:

- Set up the meeting (advise of date, room booking, refreshments, etc).
- Ensure that everyone knows where and when to attend.
- Prepare a detailed agenda.
- Ensure distribution of information (to participants, and others if necessary).
- Prepare self (read papers and previous minutes, familiarise with names, etc).

During the meeting:

- Take the minutes.

After the meeting:

- Approach the chairperson or participants to clarify any misunderstandings.

- Type up the minutes within a couple of days.
- Ensure the minutes are approved and dispatched.

Those attending the meeting

Contributors

Before the meeting:

- Request a meeting if necessary.
- Respond quickly to the invitation to the meeting.
- Send items for the agenda in good time.
- Read the agenda and accompanying papers.
- Ensure that previous actions are complete.

During the meeting:

- Arrive on time and prepared.
- Contribute appropriately (as to both time and manner).
- Keep contributions relevant to the agenda.
- Show common courtesy and respect for others' opinions.
- Note personal action points.

After the meeting:

- Complete action points within deadlines agreed.
- Read and respond to minutes.

Observers

Before the meeting:

- Ensure their purpose for attending is clear.
- Undertake any necessary preparation.

During the meeting:

- **Observe, but don't contribute.**

After the meeting:

- **Write up any necessary notes.**
- **If appropriate, give feedback to the chairperson.**

If all the participants are aware of what they have to achieve and are well briefed, and the chairperson is focused and effective, the minute-taker's task should not be difficult.

2

Arranging a meeting

In theory setting up a meeting should present no problem: a few phone calls, a confirmation note or e-mail and that's it. Anyone who has tried to do it knows the reality: endless calls trying to find mutually convenient dates, difficulty in booking rooms, and economies that mean no sandwiches and grumbling participants.

Keep an accurate and well-planned database of those who attend the meetings you set up. Since many will attend more than one meeting, it is generally best to keep one overall meeting database, rather than one for each meeting. This is typically done in Microsoft Access or Excel.

Use separate fields of first and surname (for ease of inserting the greeting), whatever contact details are necessary, and fields for job title and department (for merging into the minutes under 'Present', etc). Keep one field for a code to identify which meetings people attend; for example HS for Health & Safety, BP for Business Planning. Multiple codes can be entered for those who attend more than one meeting.

It is worth having one field called something like 'mark'. This can be used for one-off meetings; just insert a familiar symbol

in this field for everyone who is to attend and then use it to merge.

Merge with this database for address labels, circulation lists, attendance list on minutes and any other documents. Build directories in your e-mail system so that you can easily e-mail everyone who attends a meeting without having to enter individual addresses each time.

Before you begin, make sure you know who must attend, who should attend and what is needed for the meeting.

Who will attend

The regular meeting

In most cases, it is the same group that attends each meeting and the date is set at the end of the previous meeting. This is much the best way to arrange it as everyone should have diaries available. If necessary, prompt the chairperson to finish off each meeting by deciding when and where the next should be held. If this is forgotten in the rush to get out of the room, it is quite acceptable for the minute-taker to ask for the next date 'for the minutes'.

If the date of the meeting is not set, or if it has to be changed, find out whose attendance is essential: that is, their withdrawal would cause the meeting to be cancelled. These are the people with whom you should agree the date. The other participants can be offered dates at the same time (with less priority given to their choice) or simply told of the date afterwards. It is not necessary to tell them that their importance is secondary and that they have to put up with the date!

It may be that some people are essential for only some of the items to be discussed. If this is the case, these items could be deferred to the next meeting if the relevant individuals cannot attend.

Visitors

For many meetings there will be visitors who need to be invited on a one-off basis. These might be from other organisations or fellow employees, but they are not part of the group that meets regularly. Make sure you know whether visitors are needed for the whole meeting or just part of it. Make sure that visitors know:

- **why they are attending;**
- **what will be asked of them;**
- **where their involvement fits into the overall objective of the meeting;**
- **who else will be present.**

The one-off meeting

Before you begin to arrange the meeting find out who the 'priority people' are – those without whom the meeting cannot go ahead. If booking a room is likely to cause problems, this is also the time to check availability and reserve the room. Select a few dates, spreading them across different days of the week and times of the day and then e-mail or fax everyone with a 'notice of meeting', explaining why the meeting is being held and offering dates. You might also wish to insert a personal sentence explaining why each individual's attendance is requested. Make sure that you give a clear deadline for confirming attendance. Figure 2.1 gives an example e-mail notice of meeting. Note that the e-mail heading is the subject of the meeting, not 'Notice of meeting', so readers can immediately see what it is about.

Administration

Give due warning

If too little notice is given, participants will be ill-prepared. If papers have not been read, this will have to be done at the

From <dlatimer@mkthompson.co.uk.>
To: <wsmith@mkthompson.co.uk>
Sent: 12 March 2009 15:23
Subject: Resurfacing of car park

Notice of meeting

Alchemist Tarmac has gone into liquidation. We need to get together to decide what action to take and to start the process of selecting a new contractor from the tender list. I would anticipate that the meeting will last 45 minutes.

Please advise which of the following dates you are able to make:

Wednesday 18 March, 9.30 am
Wednesday 18 March, 3.00 pm
Thursday 19 March, 11.00 am
Monday 23 March, 10.30 am

Please reply by 11.00 am, Monday 16 March and the meeting date will be confirmed by 3.00 pm that same day.

David

Figure 2.1 Example e-mail notice of meeting

meeting. This not only wastes time, but comprehension is likely to be poor and readers often latch on to a point they strongly agree or disagree with. This leads to argument. If issues have not been thought through, arguing is again likely, as is a resultant poor decision.

If items are not fully discussed, or decisions are poor, the subject is likely to be raised again at the next meeting. This might be intentionally via the agenda or unintentionally because someone goes back to the subject. Inevitably the whole thing is discussed again, wasting considerable time.

There is no fixed rule for the amount of notice you should give, but ensure that it is enough for all preparation to be done, usually around a week.

Get agenda items

For a one-off meeting, the notice of meeting should ask for agenda items and give a deadline for their receipt. Anything arising after that time will be dealt with as 'Any other business'.

For regular meetings, include a deadline for agenda items under 'Date of next meeting'. Throughout the meeting, listen for items that are left with a vague, 'We'll talk about that next time', because they will need to appear on the agenda. Some agenda items will follow naturally from previous meetings and the minute-taker will need to keep track of these.

Although it should not be necessary, the minute-taker will often have to ring around, asking for items. This can be lessened by asking the chairperson to finish the next meeting by explaining the deadline and pointing out that anything received after that date won't be accepted for the agenda. Providing that the rule is enforced, participants soon get the idea that laziness won't be tolerated. Items that can be shown to have arisen after the agenda was sent out can be taken as 'Any other business' as usual.

Allow sufficient time

Few people like long meetings, and the length of time taken is a common complaint. This is sometimes the fault of the chairperson for allowing non-productive argument and not drawing items to a close, and is sometimes caused by having an unrealistic number of items for discussion.

A meeting must be long enough to allow the business to be discussed completely. When items are sent in for the agenda, ask how long is required and use this to calculate the time necessary. This has the added advantage of developing your understanding of the issues through talking to participants, which will help when taking the minutes. If there is too much to be discussed in the time available, a second meeting should be arranged or some items deferred to the following meeting. This will have to be discussed with the chairperson.

There is no maximum time for a meeting, but one lasting for more than a couple of hours is bound to have periods when concentration slips. If the meeting is scheduled to last for more than an hour and a half, schedule in a five-minute coffee stop so everyone can refresh themselves (including the minute-taker!). This also helps structure the meeting and will usually speed it up, as the break on the agenda means everyone knows that a particular point has to be reached by coffee time.

The right environment

Although there's usually not much choice, wherever possible choose a room that will be comfortable. This will make the meeting easier to chair and to minute, and it is more likely to be productive. The room size and layout should be appropriate, and the room light and airy with minimum distractions. See Chapter 6 for more information.

Refreshments

Make sure that coffee and tea are available at the start of the meeting, and encourage the chairperson to make sure that everyone has some and then have the tray taken out. This should prevent the one-by-one drift back for refills, which is distracting for all. A short 'coffee stop' should be built into longer meetings (see above). Water should be available throughout.

Equipment

Make sure you know what equipment is required by participants (eg overhead projector, flipchart), so this can be booked. It is always a good idea to have a flipchart in a meeting room, as it can be used to list ideas or problems. Listing the latter is a good way of taking the heat out of an argument; focusing on the flipchart stops people focusing on one another and slows the pace.

> ## Tip
> Prepare a master checklist of absolutely everything you might need to do. For each meeting you arrange, print off a copy and, as you set up the meeting, cross out the things that are not relevant and then tick off the tasks as you do them.

Receiving apologies

Apologies can be received at three stages:

- When the future date is set at the end of the meeting, someone may say 'I can't make it but you carry on.' This is not minuted or mentioned on the agenda for the next meeting (unless you choose to show a circulation list). However, it should be listed as an apology for the next meeting.
- At any time before the next meeting.
- Via someone else on the day.

You should also include those who know you are aware, for example, of their holiday, even if they do not specifically relate this to the meeting.

When committee members send apologies for a meeting, check whether they were responsible for any item on the agenda. If it is a general item, it can usually be dealt with in their absence but if their input is necessary, the item should be deferred to the next meeting.

It's also a good idea to check whether they had any action points on the last minutes and find out their progress, so you or the chairperson can report on their behalf at the meeting.

3

Sections of a meeting

Meetings need to be structured if they are to be effective. That is not to say that the structure has to be overt, seeming to be more important than the content. Compare it to a day in the city with your family. It is likely to be more successful if you know what you want to visit and in what order, but you can present this as either 'It's 3 o'clock, time to move on to the museum; we've been here for an hour', or 'Let's go and have a look at the museum.' One sounds like the timetable ruling the day, the second like a good idea!

Formal meetings are likely to have a more obvious structure. For informal meetings the chairperson might not want to appear so dictatorial. However, it is having an underlying plan that will keep the meeting to time and productive; the skill is to avoid drawing attention to the structure.

Some of the sections of a meeting might sound out of date or too formal to you, and most can be changed to suit specific purposes and styles. The overall process is to:

- **sort out the administration;**
- **confirm the past;**

- **deal with current issues;**
- **deal with last-minute issues;**
- **plan for the future.**

The sections of the meeting are outlined below together with suggestions for how to make them seem more modern and/or less formal. You do not need to use every section for every meeting but at least you can make an informed choice and use the ones that are appropriate. However, whichever you use, they are usually kept in this order.

Introduction/welcome

The introduction is the point where the chairperson gets the meeting under control and started. There is not usually anything to minute at this stage and it is therefore not an item that appears on the agenda.

There may be a general introduction for the benefit of some or all of the participants. If there is a 'round-the-table' introduction, make notes of names in the form of a table plan to help during the meeting. It is worth watching out for 'substitutions': people who have come in place of those you expected.

Occasionally the introduction is used for a specific purpose worth minuting and if this is planned it should appear on the agenda.

Apologies

'Apologies' is the opportunity to clarify who is, and is not, at the meeting. The names of those who have said they will not attend are usually given by the chairperson or secretary, but others may be added by participants.

It is the minute-taker's responsibility to get an accurate list of who is present, who is substituting, who has apologised and who has simply failed to turn up. To keep the list complete, be

aware of who sits on the committee and make this your starting point rather than noting those attending and names mentioned.

Declarations of interest

There may be an item on the agenda to which a participant cannot contribute because of some conflicting interest. There should be a rule laid down for this (whether the individual should leave the meeting or just cannot contribute to the item), but if it is a one-off situation, the group may need to decide the appropriate approach. This section is common in local government but less so elsewhere.

Committee business

This section is for business that relates to the committee rather than to its purpose in meeting. It is likely to involve changes to the:

- *structure*, **for example:**
 - **discussion on how a committee should be made up;**
 - **changes to take into account a merger with another organisation.**
- *function*, **for example:**
 - **changes to the remit of the group;**
 - **discussion as to whether the group still has a purpose;**
 - **confirmation that a part of the group's work is no longer necessary.**
- *personnel*, **for example:**
 - **resignations and new members joining;**
 - **long-term substitutions (to cover maternity or sabbatical periods);**
 - **confirmation of roles within the group.**

- *administration*, for example:
 - a change of chairperson;
 - alteration of frequency of meetings from monthly to quarterly;
 - change of venue from always at head office to a rotation between divisional offices;
 - the possibility of doing without 'Any other business'.

This is a main business item and should always be minuted in the same style as the rest of the minutes. If there is more than one item you can list them as subheadings under the main heading of 'Committee business' or as sequential items with relevant headings.

To make committee business sound more modern, give it a relevant title (eg 'Administration', 'Resignation', 'Long-term future of [name] group').

Minutes of previous meeting

Although it can seem that this section is designed solely to humiliate the minute-taker, there are actually two reasons for having it. The first is to *confirm that the minutes are accurate.* Time should not be wasted with corrections to grammar and punctuation; it is the errors of fact that should be noted (eg showing £5,000 as £5,500 may be a typing mistake, but it has the appearance of fact and is worth minuting).

The second reason is to *prevent individuals changing the minutes without the knowledge of the group.* If you take corrections from individuals you may end up with conflicting changes. More importantly, people will be changing the minutes without the knowledge of the rest of the group and the final copy will not be the one that everyone has seen. The chairperson should draw attention to changes already notified and individuals should add any other points. That way, changes can be debated and will be clearly shown in the minutes.

Minutes are seldom signed these days. If they are, it is done

by the chairperson at the meeting. The purpose of signing is to demonstrate further that everyone at the meeting signalled their acceptance of the content – the chairperson signs on behalf of the other participants. If the minutes are not bound, they should be signed on the front cover and initialled on every other page.

Time is often wasted on this part of the meeting, either because participants start reading the minutes or because the chairperson guides them through, page by page. With this approach, people are looking for 'mistakes' so it is no surprise that they make changes. They will also spot things to talk about and start unnecessary discussion, and may give feedback on actions and other things that have happened since the last meeting.

In order for this section of the meeting to run efficiently, the minutes should have been read before attending. The chairperson should assume this and just ask for any amendments. If people start reading, the item can be deferred to the next meeting, to 'allow everyone time to read the minutes'.

The heading for this section seldom changes, but you can use headings like 'Confirmation of minutes' or 'Approval of minutes'; you can change 'previous' to 'last'; or you can include the date: 'Minutes of the meeting held on [date]'.

Matters arising

'Matters arising' is often one of the most chaotic parts of a meeting because participants are reading through the minutes and end up repeating the arguments of the previous meeting (see Chapter 4 for advice on how to prevent this). Another common problem is an individual boring the meeting by describing in detail how the action point was completed.

'Matters arising' is an important part of the meeting, the confirmation that actions have been completed. There is little point in having actions if there is no record that these actions have been completed. During the section, individuals who took responsibility for any action that falls due by this meeting should

be required to confirm that they have completed their work. If they have encountered problems, the group can advise and the action point may change.

If some of the action points relate to items that are also on the agenda, the relevant 'Matters arising' can be incorporated in those items. Make sure it is clear on the agenda what is an action to be followed up and what is business for discussion at the meeting (see Figure 3.1). There may be a general item in previous minutes on which the group needs an update. This can also be included in 'Matters arising'.

6. **Open day**

 6.1 **Matters arising**

 (a) Delivery of furniture for Year 9 classes

 (b) Availability of sports centre

 6.2 **Catering**

 6.3 **Musical performances**

Figure 3.1 Example incorporating 'Matters arising' into agenda item

Occasionally a whole meeting is justifiably 'Matters arising'. This is usually in project-planning-type events where each member is responsible for a particular aspect of the project. In this situation there should not be a separate section, but each agenda item should start with the matters arising for that subject before moving on to discuss current concerns and finishing with confirmation of the participant's next action(s). If there is new business it is usually taken after the regular items, and for the next meeting is included in the above process for the relevant person.

It is the minute-taker's responsibility to be aware of the action points due for completion and to listen carefully for information on whether or not they have been finished.

If you don't like the formal title, try 'Update on action points' or similar.

Reports

Reports are like matters arising in that they are not for debate, just to hear (or 'receive'). It may be that every participant reports on recent work (eg at a team leaders' meeting); or that just a few members have to report (eg finance report, health and safety report); or it can be a one-off. This latter type is when a member wants to give information to the rest of the group (eg reporting back from a conference).

If a report is the first part of an item, for example the conference report-back precedes discussion on implementing the best practice learnt, it is not a 'report' but a main agenda item that the individual will start.

For a meeting, the most common problem with reports is their being given out and read on the day. It is difficult to take in detail when reading in a group and time is wasted with an argument often following as individuals focus on one point they have noticed. Encourage all participants to submit reports in time to be circulated with the agenda. This can sometimes be achieved by the chairperson refusing to accept reports that were not circulated in time. Offenders usually manage to make the deadline next time!

There is no need to minute a report if a paper copy is provided. Just attach the copy to the minutes. A verbal report should be summarised for the minute-taker by the person giving it and included in the minutes.

Alternative headings include 'For information', 'Information only', 'Information items', 'Updates' or 'Correspondence'.

Agenda items

Although there have been several sections before the group gets down to the main business of the day, they should not take long. The main agenda items are the topics that group members have asked to be discussed at the meeting.

Any other business

This section allows for last-minute items to be discussed. 'Last minute' means things that happened after the agenda was dispatched and not things that a participant could not be bothered to submit. Sometimes an item may be held for any other business because the person raising it wants to discuss it without the others being prepared. This should be prevented by the chairperson – if the group members are not in a position to discuss something knowledgeably, that item should be deferred to the next meeting.

A good chairperson will begin the meeting by including a request for items for any other business in the introduction. This means that items can be slotted into the agenda where appropriate, accepted for discussion under any other business, deferred to the next meeting or rejected as not relevant to the objectives of the group. This approach gives everyone warning of what will be discussed and generally saves time.

As minute-taker you need to minute what is discussed and take note of items that are deferred to the next meeting so these can be included on the agenda.

Very occasionally, this section is called 'Late items' or 'Last-minute items'.

Date of next meeting

The purpose of this section is as it sounds – to confirm the details of the next meeting. It is always best to do this at the meeting because it takes so long to arrange dates afterwards.

4

Agenda

There are several reasons for having an agenda:

- **to enable participants to prepare for the meeting;**
- **to ensure that everything important is dealt with;**
- **to guide through subjects in a logical order;**
- **to remind the chairperson of what to discuss;**
- **to make chairing easier through everyone being aware of the structure and order;**
- **to give structure to the minutes.**

It isn't easy to fit preparing the agenda into a busy schedule and, as a result, it is often not ready till the morning of the meeting. This means the participants will not be prepared and the result will be ill-thought-out debate, argument and poor decisions.

It is vital to spend time putting together a useful agenda and you should ensure that it is well structured and reasonable for the time available. Your efforts will be rewarded by a shorter, more structured meeting. Taking the minutes becomes easier and the time involved in typing them up is much reduced. The agenda should be circulated a week before the meeting.

The deadline for agenda items should be confirmed in the previous minutes under 'Date of next meeting' and the chairperson encouraged to refuse items that are not received by that date. It is essential that any papers that need to be read before the meeting are received in time to be circulated with the agenda.

Who receives the agenda

The agenda should be sent to all participants and, as a general rule, to those who are attending for the one meeting (in part or in whole) and observers. This is a courtesy and is not essential if there are concerns about confidentiality.

Source of agenda items

Agenda items come from two primary sources: the chairperson and the committee members. Although it would be helpful to receive agenda items without asking for them, this is seldom the case and the minute-taker ends up nagging participants for topics they want to discuss.

Layout

The basic layout of the agenda does not vary greatly from one organisation to another. It is essential that it includes the name of the group that is to meet, the date, time and place of the meeting, and the headings of the different agenda items. It may also be necessary to give a contact name and number for apologies and, if the group is not a regular committee, a list of those invited to attend – a circulation list.

Heading

The heading can be either the more traditional paragraph

style (see Figure 4.1), or the more modern centred style (see Figure 4.2).

Giving a closing time is a matter of preference, but doing so means everyone knows how long the meeting should take.

Agenda for the IT User Group meeting to be held on 23 June 2009 from 10.30 to 12.00 in meeting room 6, Emmerson House.

Figure 4.1 Paragraph-style heading

IT User Group Meeting

23 June 2009, 10.30–12.00
Meeting Room 6, Emmerson House

AGENDA

Figure 4.2 Centred heading

Agenda styles

There are three styles of agenda; each has its use and it is worth considering which is best for your meetings.

Basic agenda

The basic agenda is by far the most common style in use today; sadly it is also the least effective. The headings tend to be quite vague and as a result participants could discuss their interests or concerns under more than one heading, so subjects will almost

Facilities and Administration Committee

29 May 2009, 3.30 pm, Meeting room 3

Agenda

Apologies

1. Administration

2. Minutes of the previous meeting

3. Matters arising

4. Reports

5. Visit of David Smith MP

6. Smoking room

7. Canteen

8. Post delivery

9. Any other business

10. Date of next meeting

Figure 4.3 Basic agenda

inevitably get discussed twice (or more). The general heading means that people will have different ideas of what needs to be covered under a heading, so the discussion is likely to be muddled and some aspects may be left out altogether. An example of the basic agenda is given in Figure 4.3.

A basic agenda is useful for meetings where everyone is clear exactly what the headings mean and what type of outcome is required for each. This is almost always a project-planning or

report-back type of meeting where the same headings are used each month.

Full agenda

A full agenda gives more detailed information, specifically as detailed in the following sections.

Subheadings

- *For matters arising*
 As minute-taker you are responsible for keeping track of when action points become due for report-back. Many of these will be at the next meeting, but sometimes there is a longer timescale. On the agenda, list each action point that is due for completion by this meeting – usually to give the heading is enough – and add the name or initials of the person responsible. This will enable the chairperson to work through the list, ensuring that every action is complete. This approach also reminds people of their actions and means they look at the agenda rather than the previous minutes, which will reduce the amount of time spent repeating the arguments of the last meeting (see Figure 4.4).

2. **Matters arising**
 2.1 Workforce reform timetable (4.0)
 2.2 Cover for Mrs Maitland's maternity leave (6.2)
 2.3 Replacement of climbing frame (9.4)
 2.4 Cycle proficiency training (10.0)

Figure 4.4 'Matters arising' with subheadings

Note: the numbers after the headings relate to the agenda/ minute numbers in the previous minutes.

- *For reports*
 Simply number and list the topics for reports and the name or initials of the person reporting.
- *For main agenda items*
 If the heading is too general it allows anything and everything to be discussed, and often an important aspect is left out. For example, in Figure 4.3, there is the heading of 'Visit of David Smith MP'. Figure 4.5 demonstrates this heading with subheadings. By dividing it in this way, everyone can see what is to be discussed and is therefore more likely to wait for the right moment, rather than interrupting with their thoughts throughout the discussion. The subheadings also mean that every necessary aspect of items will be discussed, rather than just those that occur to the participants.

```
5.    Visit of David Smith MP
      5.1   Timetable
      5.2   Publicity
      5.3   Security
```

Figure 4.5 Heading with subheadings

As minute-taker you will not necessarily be able to prepare the subheadings. It may have to be done in consultation with the chairperson or the individuals who submit items. In fact this is an advantage in many cases and you will be better prepared to take the minutes as a result of such consultation. Figure 4.6 shows an example of a full agenda.

Facilities and Administration Committee

29 May 2009, 3.30 pm, Meeting room 3

Agenda

Notes

Apologies

1. Administration

2. Minutes of the previous meeting

3. Matters arising
 3.1. Canteen tables D Simmonds
 3.2 Menu boards M Daniels
 3.3 Car park lighting T Young

4. Reports
 4.1 Health and safety annual review R Budgeon
 4.2 Staff forum D Simmonds
 4.3 Administrative management course R Davies

5. Visit of David Smith MP
 5.1 Timetable draft attached R Davis
 5.2 Publicity R Budgeon
 5.3 Security T Young

6. Smoking room

7. Canteen
 7.1 Redecoration
 7.2 Chairs brochure attached D Simmonds
 7.3 Reading material

8. Post delivery
 8.1 Problems following merger
 8.2 Delivery frequency consult colleagues

9. Any other business

10. Date of next meeting

Figure 4.6 Full agenda

Notes of papers that are attached

Any papers that are to be read before the meeting must be sent out with the agenda and should be listed by the relevant agenda items. This column can be headed 'Papers', 'Reports' or 'Attached'.

Instructions/guidance

If participants are required to undertake any action or consultation before the meeting, this can also be listed by the relevant item. This can be in the same column as the papers, in which case the heading is usually 'Notes' (papers are listed as 'Paper attached').

Lead speakers

Many items will start with specific input from a participant, either a formal report or an informal update or explanation. Where this is the case, show the name on the agenda. This gives the chairperson guidance on who to turn to, and prevents participants making too early a contribution (possibly having misunderstood the subject).

Where the item is for general discussion, do not put a name, even if one person highlighted the need to discuss it. If that person has nothing specific to say, time will be wasted if he or she rambles on.

Names must be placed alongside items in Matters Arising and Reports (showing who was responsible for the action and who is to report).

Objectives agenda

In an objectives agenda, the subheadings for main business items are replaced by objectives. This gives clearer guidance as to what has to be achieved (rather than what is to be discussed). Figure 4.7 gives the heading for the MP's visit in this form.

..

5. Visit of David Smith MP
 5.1 To confirm timetable for visit
 5.2 To agree strategy for maximising publicity
 5.3 To discuss security implications of visit

..

Figure 4.7 Heading with objectives

Although objectives can be given for the administrative items, this is usually thought to be overly wordy and may appear patronising. It is clearest to use them where they serve a specific purpose. However, it is important to be consistent. If you decide to use objectives, they must be given for each main business item or there will be undue emphasis on those with objectives. If there would be one heading and no subheadings (if it were a full agenda), there will be one objective. Where there would be three subheadings (if it were a full agenda), there will be a heading and three objectives. This will again involve consultation in many cases.

Remember that these objectives will need to be given as subheadings in the minutes and you should bear this in mind when deciding the wording. Figure 4.8 shows an example of an objectives agenda.

Useful words

There are some phrases that come in useful for an objectives agenda, and you will no doubt find more. Choose the word that is most appropriate for the type of discussion or outcome necessary:

	where the group are to:
to receive	be told (eg a report)
to decide*	decide the outcome at this meeting
to agree*	agree the outcome at this meeting
	(ie the same as decide)

to confirm	confirm an earlier choice or the choice of another group
to approve	approve an earlier choice or the choice of another group (ie the same as confirm)
to discuss	talk about
to select*	choose between alternatives
to establish	find out
to resolve*	sort out (usually a problem)
to explore	talk about (ie the same as discuss)

*items that use these words are required to result in an action point. However, any other objective may result in an action point if that proves the appropriate outcome.

With an objectives agenda you know where decisions are required, and it is considerably easier to listen for them and, if necessary, remind the chairperson of the necessity to decide.

A logical order for agenda items

A group that jumps from one agenda item to another and back again causes great problems for the minute-taker, but sometimes the fault lies in a poorly designed agenda.

There is no 'right' order, but it is generally preferable to deal with important items first. This is to help achieve useful discussion while everyone is fresh and focused and also in case time runs short at the end.

Look out for items that are closely linked and should follow one another or those that are basically the same and can be incorporated as one item, perhaps with subheadings.

If some people will have to do a lot of talking, it may help to split their agenda items to give them a rest and to give others a change of voice to listen to.

Facilities and Administration Committee

29 May 2009, 3.30 pm, Meeting room 3

Agenda

Apologies

1. Administration
 To review arrangements for minute taking

2. Minutes of the previous meeting

3. Matters arising
 3.1. Canteen tables D Simmonds
 3.2 Menu boards M Daniels
 3.3 Car park lighting T Young

4. Reports
 4.1 Health and safety annual review R Budgeon
 4.2 Staff forum D Simmonds
 4.3 Administrative management course R Davies

5. Visit of David Smith MP
 5.1 To confirm timetable for visit draft R Davis
 attached

 5.2 To agree strategy for maximising publicity R Budgeon
 5.3 To discuss security implications of visit T Young .

6. Outdoor smoking area
 To decide future of outdoor smoking area

7. Canteen
 7.1 To draw up plans for redecoration
 7.2 To confirm style of chairs brochure D Simmonds
 attached

 7.3 To discuss provision of consult
 reading material colleagues

8. Post delivery
 8.1 To consider problems following merger
 8.2 To agree standards for delivery frequency consult
 colleagues

9. Any other business

10. Date of next meeting

Figure 4.8 Example objectives agenda

Timing the agenda

Some groups find that including times for items on the agenda is worthwhile. If you do this, use real time (10.15, 10.35) rather than time allowed (20 minutes, 15 minutes), so that it is easy to judge whether the meeting is on time.

Timing the agenda means that everyone can see how much time is allowed and gives an indication of the relative importance of each item. It also enables the chairperson to use the excuse of 'not much time' to quieten a dominant group member in a less personal or aggressive way than asking that member to be quiet.

Ask those with agenda items how long they need for the discussion (without giving any guarantee that they will have that time!). This means that you can assess the amount of time needed before the meeting starts and address any problem of shortage of time. This has the added advantage of reminding participants that time is important.

Timing the agenda serves little purpose when ignored by the chairperson and participants, so is only worth the effort if used.

Use headings and numbering

When you decide on headings for the agenda items, choose wording that will indicate to participants exactly what will be discussed.

The agenda items should be numbered with sub-numbering where appropriate (see the examples above). Keep a copy of the agenda in front of you throughout the meeting so that you can reference in your notes any item taken out of place or duplicated, by its number.

If you plan to present 'Apologies' at the top of the minutes, alongside 'Present', make sure it is not numbered on the agenda or everything will be out of order by one number.

Layout and presentation

The agenda is the advertisement for your meeting. If it looks
scruffy and unprofessional, you will discourage those you want
to attend. It should be presented so that the page does not look
overcrowded, with headings sized in relation to their relative
importance, appropriate widths for columns and so on. The
examples above give an indication as to the generally preferred
layout.

A circulation list

If the same group attend each meeting, there is no point in
showing a circulation list. If someone is to attend for a specific
item, this can be shown on the agenda (see Figure 4.9). If the
meeting is a one-off event, or if there are several visitors,
consider whether it is worth indicating who will be attending.

8.	**Post delivery**
	Irene Maddox, Post Room Manager, will attend
8.1	To consider problems following merger
8.2	To agree standards for
	delivery frequency consult colleagues

Figure 4.9 Example showing visitor to meeting

If the agenda is being circulated to external visitors, it may be
worth showing who attends for their benefit. If you prefer, this
can be done as a separate note.

Chairperson's brief

This is just a more detailed agenda, drawn up to help the chairperson manage the meeting. It will highlight exactly what is required from each section, how long to allow for it and any other information that will help, including background briefing notes if necessary.

The brief is hardly ever used today, apart from for the most formal of meetings, but it could help a less experienced chairperson or one who has little time to prepare.

The minute-taker and chairperson should get together for a few minutes to discuss the meeting, flag any potential problems and agree how the meeting will run. Although this is seldom a formal meeting, it is a valuable aid to minute taking and helps remind the chairperson of the importance of your role.

5

Personal preparation

It is difficult to find time to prepare for a meeting; it is often a case of finishing the phone call and dashing in. Of course you may not even know that you are to minute the meeting. Plenty of people think 'anyone' or 'any secretary' can take the minutes and you might find yourself called in with no notice. Despite the difficulties, time spent on preparation is usually recouped at the meeting and afterwards when typing the minutes.

Read the agenda

Rather than just skimming over the subjects, read through each item and consider what will be discussed, what terminology will be used and so on. If you identify any problem areas, it is quite acceptable to ring or meet to get background information or any other help you need. Just raising awareness of your concerns may encourage others to be sensitive to your difficulties.

Read the papers

Ideally, you should be able to find the time to read papers in depth so you are familiar with the language and the content. In reality, it is more likely that you will only have time to scan them. At least do this, as you will then know what type of information is there and may pick up details to help you at the meeting.

Talk to the chairperson

Meet with the chairperson, either formally or informally, to discuss what is to be covered, where decisions are expected, what style of minutes is required and how you are required to behave (eg can you interrupt?). This is also your opportunity to ask for any specific help or general guidance you may need.

Talk to the contributors

It is not enough to understand the words on the agenda; you have to know the context. For example, you might understand the words 'Holiday cover for support staff' but you need to know which holiday. Who do people think should provide the cover? What's the budget likely to be? How many are needed? And so on. It may be that the person who has raised the subject has no idea, and that is why it is on the agenda, but often people do have some thoughts and it is useful to be aware of them.

Rather than ask specific questions and find you have misunderstood the words, start with something general (you could ask: could you give me some background? Why is it an issue? Are you looking for a decision at the meeting?). You can always follow up with specific questions if you need to. You will also often pick up useful abbreviations or acronyms at this stage which will help in the meeting.

Talk to others

If there is an 'expert' who can help you with information on any
agenda item you particularly fear, take the trouble to ask for help.

Consider who's who

In terms of knowing who you will be working with, meeting
participants are likely to fall into three groups:

1. Those you know well (you'd recognise them out of context,
 for example in the supermarket). You don't need to give
 any further thought to these.
2. Those you've met, but would struggle to recognise out of
 context. Before the meeting, remind yourself of what they
 look like, consciously putting name to face in your mind.
 This will enable you to recognise them as soon as you see
 them and you will find it easier to remember their names
 when taking the minutes.
3. Those you haven't met. Try to find out what they look like
 by asking colleagues. Even if you cannot get any
 information, you have narrowed these to a smaller, more
 manageable group, and can approach them and introduce
 yourself promptly on the day. If you find it difficult to talk
 to strangers, plan a couple of open questions (those that
 start with what, where, when, how or who) to get the
 person chatting.

Confirm the administrative arrangements

If the arrival of coffee or booking of equipment is a problem in
your organisation, double-check the arrangements – much
less stressful than wondering if something will arrive as
planned.

Remind reception of visitors to your meeting

You should meet visitors who are attending the whole meeting – a good chance to establish personal contact. Those who are coming in for one item only can be directed as you wish.

Get the equipment together

Make sure that you have enough paper, suitable pens or pencils, a clipboard if there is no table, the attendance list and your copy of the agenda and papers. You might also want a copy of the last minutes (or even earlier ones) and spare agenda and minutes for those who have forgotten theirs. It is also worth taking the phone numbers of anyone you might have to call: to tell them that it's time to come in, to locate the coffee, etc.

Signed minutes

If the minutes are to be signed, take a copy to the meeting. This is the 'file' copy, not yours or the chairperson's. Even if minutes are not to be signed, and they seldom are, it may help to take a copy of the minutes to amend if there are changes – it's quicker than writing them out in your notes.

Last-minute minute-taker

Personal preparation is certainly recommended, but is not possible if you are called in at the last minute. Assuming you cannot refuse, say that you are happy to help and immediately ask for the help you will need. This is usually one or all of the following, but you can ask for more if you want:

- sight of the agenda and a verbal explanation of the headings;

Meeting checklist

☐ I have read and thought through the agenda

☐ I have read/skimmed the papers

☐ I have spoken to contributors to understand the context of items

☐ I know where decisions are expected

☐ I've discussed the meeting with the chairperson

☐ I know what style of minutes I'm writing

☐ I've booked tea/coffee/lunch

☐ I've arranged:

 ☐ overhead projector

 ☐ flipchart (and paper/pens)

 ☐ equipment for computer presentations

 ☐ extension leads

☐ Reception knows who's expected

☐ I know the names of those I haven't met

☐ I've thought of a couple of subjects for conversations with 'strangers'

☐ I've double-checked the administrative arrangements

I've got:

☐ paper

☐ pens/pencils

☐ clipboard

☐ the agenda

☐ copies of the papers

☐ minutes for my reference

☐ minutes for signing

☐ spare copies of minutes

☐ spare copies of the agenda

Figure 5.1 Example meeting checklist

- **guidance on the depth and style of minutes required;**
- **introduction to the participants;**
- **ongoing summarising.**

It is quite acceptable to point out that you do not have a full knowledge of the subject but make your voice tone warm and strong so that it does not sound as though you are incompetent or whingeing.

Personal preparation checklist

To save yourself time, prepare a checklist that can be printed off and used for all meetings. You can use the checklist in Figure 5.1 or prepare one that meets your needs.

6

Creating the right environment

Having booked a room, it is likely that there will still be some work to do to make it ready for the meeting, to create a businesslike impression and to help yourself in the minute-taking role.

Present a businesslike first impression

Make sure that the room is tidy, with chairs neatly arranged, papers ready and so on. Although it is unlikely that anyone will consciously notice, subconsciously it sends a strong message of 'place for business'. If it looks like a coffee lounge, it will be treated as one.

Freshen the room

If possible, open a window for a few minutes so that the room is aired. Turn on the lights so that the room looks like a good place to work.

Layout

There should be an obvious 'head of table' position for the chairperson and yourself. This should be at the narrow end of a rectangular table or oval table. If the table is round create a head position by giving a little extra space between you and the chairperson, and the remainder of the chairs. If the table is square, do not place a chair at the front of each side as those people will struggle to catch the chairperson's eye. Everyone should be able to have eye contact with the chairperson (and you with them to aid your hearing).

Do not allow yourself to be sidelined to a table or chair away from the main group. It is essential for your ability to hear (not to mention your status) that you are at the table. You should also make sure you take your place next to the chairperson. A large part of the discussion is focused in this direction and it is difficult to hear if looking at the backs of heads. If you need eye contact with the chairperson, stay at the front, but at a right angle – the first person along the side.

Make sure that your 'head of table' position is not near an air-conditioning unit or other barrier to hearing.

Make sure that there is a chair for everyone and that they are neither too cramped nor too spread out.

Refreshments

If possible, have water on the table. It is preferable to have coffee at a separate table so everyone can help themselves. Try to have space for a brief pre-meeting chat and make sure that you are part of that, getting to know people and presenting yourself as a confident member of the team.

Check equipment

Although there is no reason for you to be expert on the workings

of an overhead projector, it is surprising how many people turn to the minute-taker when the lead won't reach the plug. Make sure that all equipment is working, screens and flipcharts can be seen, there are adequate marker pens, etc. After all, you are the one likely to be sent for help if there is a problem and that makes minuting impossible.

Extra copies of papers

As many minute-takers will testify, a significant percentage of meeting participants turn up without the papers they need. This is even more irritating when they swear they did not receive the copy that you personally delivered. However, it is much easier to take extra copies than be sent out to the copier.

It should only be necessary to take spare copies of the agenda as this is essential for the meeting. Spare copies of previous minutes should not be necessary: participants should have read them for errors before the meeting and actions should be listed on the agenda for feedback under Matters Arising. Provided you have your reference set, no one else should need his or her copy.

Be there to greet

It is much more comfortable to be in the room to greet people, rather than rushing in when everyone has arrived, particularly if they are already seated. This will help you put names to faces, meet those who are new to you and generally present yourself as a confident member of the team – the host role. If you fail and have to walk into the room after everyone has sat down, open the door steadily and close it behind you to give yourself time to look around the room and choose your place. You may be feeling embarrassed, but make sure your body language is confident and poised.

Mobiles and pagers

Make sure that all mobiles and pagers are turned off (you may need the chairperson to ask for this). For those who cannot bear to be out of contact, try to find a colleague who sits near the meeting room to 'mind' the machines, field calls and only interrupt for issues of life or death. Ensure that the chairperson asks those taking a call to leave the room.

Less seriously, but equally effectively, have a £1 fine for every interruption, with takings to an appropriate charity!

7

Attending the meeting

Many minute-takers do not like attending a meeting. Quite apart from the difficulties of taking notes, they are uncomfortable within the group, often feeling out of place.

If, as minute-taker, you are respected by the group and treated well by them, this chapter is not for you. For a great many people, attending the meeting as a mute or non-contributing minute-taker can be daunting, particularly when working with a new group.

You would be unlucky to suffer from all the problems below, but most people have encountered one or two. Most of the problems stem from a less-than-competent chairperson, one who lets the meeting leave the agenda, allows the loud to dominate and fails to draw in the quiet. Most difficult of all for the minute-taker is the chairperson who does not summarise the discussion (in fact this can cause problems for all the participants).

Where to sit

Some groups ostracise the minute-taker, even to the point of making him or her sit at a separate table. On other occasions it is the minute-taker who would rather be invisible and hides in the corner. As minute-taker, you are part of the 'management team' for the meeting and your place is next to the chairperson.

Claim your seat

Make sure that you get to the room early to reserve your seat. If you work for an organisation where everyone wants to sit by the chairperson, leave something personal in your place – an old purse with a bit of change in it or some car keys. People will move papers, a briefcase and even a handbag, but only the seriously determined will pick up someone's purse or wallet.

Finding out who's who

It is your responsibility to produce an accurate note of who attends the meeting and this can be difficult if you do not know everyone who attends. Although you are unlikely to have to put names or initials in minutes, it will probably help your recall of the meeting to have names in your notes. If you don't know who someone is, there are a number of things to try:

- *Use an attendance sheet*
 To avoid people signing, use a typed 'blank table' rather than a sheet of A4. Divide it into columns for the information you need, typically name (a column each for title, first name and surname) and department or organisation. You may also want an address and phone number or e-mail. If they still sign their names, add a first column for signature – most people will print after signing. You may find it helps to wait until everyone is seated and then pass the sheet around – you then get

the names in order and can refer to someone by his or her seating position in your notes and work out the name later. For a larger meeting print the sheet on bright paper to prevent its getting stuck as it moves around the table. People will notice it!

- *Use name cards or labels*
 If you put out A5 cards, folded in half lengthways, and a few flipchart pens, most people will write their names without thinking about it. If this is not feasible, type a sheet of sticky labels with the names large enough to be read at a distance (unlike most identification badges). These can be given out on arrival or passed around. It is generally not advisable to plan the seating positions by placing name cards. People usually sit with their colleagues but don't think to move the cards. If this is the case for your meetings and you want preprinted cards, just keep them by the door to collect on arrival.
- *Ask someone*
 It is always better to ask at the meeting because other people may not remember what someone looked like or what he or she was wearing.
- *Listen for clues*
 People will often give clues, saying things like 'How's life in Birmingham?' If you have prepared by reading through your list of likely attendees, you may well be able to work out who is who in this way. Even more obvious, listen for strangers being called by their name and you should be able to work out who each is.
- *Ask the stranger*
 It is not easy to approach people to find out who they are – it feels somewhat rude. However, it is a useful thing to do because it gives you a chance to familiarise yourself with their speech pattern. It also gives you the chance to present yourself as a confident professional. For your own comfort, don't leave anything to chance. Just saying 'Hello' does not exactly start a conversation. Trying to probe with questions like 'What's happening

in your office?' may not bring the information you need.
Introducing yourself is often met with a simple 'Hello',
which again does not help. It is up to you to control the
situation, and the best way is to introduce yourself and
then ask directly for the name: 'Hello, I'm Sally, the
minute-taker today. Please could I have your name?'
Have a pad to take a note of the name and then stay to
chat for a few minutes or, if the person obviously does
not want this, you can just thank him or her and move
on. You are there in an administrative role and people
expect you to administrate!

Remembering the name

Never tell yourself that you are dreadful with names – you'll
come to believe your own negative publicity. Names are a
problem because we seldom tie the name and the face together.
We talk about people by name when they are not there, and we
look at them in conversation but without using their name. We
don't tie the two together. Try two simple techniques to help
yourself:

1. Having asked for the name, use it once or at most twice in
 conversation or in thanking the person:
 – 'How long have you worked there, *Mr Hardacre*?'
 – 'Have you been to these meetings before, *Barbara*?'
 – 'Thank you, *Mrs Ratcliffe*.'
 Don't use the name more than twice or you will sound
 insincere.
2. When you are not taking notes, either before the meeting
 or, for example, whilst people are arguing, look at each
 individual in turn and remind yourself of his or her name.
 Work round from one side of the table and, every time you
 get stuck, check with your attendance sheet and go back to
 start at the beginning. The important thing is to combine
 looking at the person whilst saying his or her name (in
 your head, of course).

For all of these, it will help if you have studied the list of likely attendees and familiarised yourself with their names. It is easy to mishear a name if you are not prepared, and you will need to be alert for those who are substituting. If you hear or are given a name you do not recognise, you can then immediately ask whether that person is taking someone's place.

Not understanding

It is very uncomfortable to sit in a meeting with the subject matter going 'over your head'. In fact, it is not just the minute-taker who suffers from this. The various experts in the room may not understand one another, but no-one likes to admit it. This can lead to some strange discussion and often to argument. As your experience with a group develops, understanding becomes less of a problem, but meanwhile there are some things you can do.

Before the meeting
If you spot something that worries you on the agenda, contact the person who wants to discuss it and ask for help. You might want to meet to discuss it, get hold of some background reading or ask for help afterwards – whatever suits you. You will also raise awareness of the potential problem and, it is hoped, the person will make things extra clear for you.

During the meeting
You should interrupt and ask for clarification. Useful questions include, 'Please could you:

- **clarify...?'**
- **explain...?'**
- **put that in layperson's terms?'**
- **summarise...?'**

If possible, talk to people at the meeting, rather than wait a few days before ringing them. It's best to sort out problems while memories are fresh.

If interrupting is not appropriate, always make a note of what you don't understand. For example, 'He's talking about the IT problem that caused the crash last week', or 'She's explaining the process for the capital planning meetings.'

See Chapter 16 on building confidence for help with actually doing this.

After the meeting

If your problem is with facts, it is quite acceptable to talk to the relevant individual. However, beware of asking someone approachable for help in understanding an argument or discussion – you will get that person's view and run the risk of bias in the minutes. You should only approach the chairperson in cases like this.

Hearing

Reduce or remove any external noise by shutting windows or closing doors. Make sure that you can see everyone to establish eye contact where necessary and, again, sit by the chairperson because discussion usually slants that way. Try to arrange the table to avoid encouraging subgroups forming. For example, a long boardroom table will often encourage those at the end to start a different conversation, as will a table that is too wide/ square, when those on the corners will chat.

Minuting an argument

Many minute-takers panic and scribble furiously as argument breaks out. These notes are then discarded because the personal views and often inappropriate tone of the discussion do not appear in the minutes.

When discussion degenerates into argument, make a careful note of what is being 'discussed' and, if you want, add some extra information that you think will be useful; then stop and rest until order is returned.

Figure 7.1 illustrates the notes taken by a minute-taker during a 20-minute argument on whether to merge two departments. The minute-taker resumed taking full notes when the chairperson brought the meeting under control.

> *Merge admin and facilities?*
> - *cost or saving?*
> - *not space to sit as one department*
> - *traditional bad feeling between them*
> - *who will be responsible?*

Figure 7.1 Example of notes taken during an argument

Skivvying

One of the most demeaning things to happen to a minute-taker is being sent out to photocopy or chase up the coffee. Quite apart from the negative message this sends, it is impossible to take notes when not in the room. It is difficult to refuse without seeming rude, so the best approach is to pass the minutes to someone else. This should be done warmly but with a clear message of 'Please could you take notes while I'm out of the room?' The ideal person to pass to is the chairperson because he or she is the one who has the power to send someone else next time.

Coping with numbers/figures

Although it might be risky to say that you should not take notes of figures at all, this is a good general rule. Figures are hard to write accurately and even if you do have them correctly in your notes, you are likely to find a page of numbers and have no idea what they mean. Figures are like stories: they are given to make a point. Someone may give statistics over the past three years but the point is, for example, that the rise in redundancies is high/slight/tailing-off/increasing. It is better to understand, and note, the point – if you want the figures for the minutes, you can always ask for them later.

Maintaining concentration and focus

Few people mean to daydream; it is more common to 'come to' and realise that you have been thinking about something else. This usually happens when you do not understand fully or when the group are repeatedly going over the same points. Sometimes though, the cause is the opposite: getting too involved in the content and forgetting that you are there to take the notes.

Light and air
Make sure that the room is well lit and well ventilated. The latter may conflict with the need to close windows to cut out noise – consider the best balance for you in any particular room.

Temperature
Try not to let the room get too hot. If you think this is likely to be a problem, wear layers of clothes that you can shed with dignity.

Maximise understanding
It is much easier to concentrate when you understand what is

being discussed, so make sure that you have read the previous minutes, the agenda and any relevant papers. If necessary, you can ask for guidance at the meeting if you feel out of your depth (see Chapter 16 on confidence for more help).

Refreshments

Keep to your normal levels of tea or coffee, but it is cold water that is most helpful in keeping you awake.

Remain part of the meeting

Sit forward, looking at those who are speaking so that you feel involved in what is going on.

Stay focused

Whether you lose focus because of daydreaming or getting involved, help yourself by sitting up with your pen ready to write. Although you must look up when a new person takes over the discussion, and eye contact is useful, generally keep your ears on the discussion, your brain on the meaning and your eyes on what you are writing. When you are not writing, look up but keep your hand ready. Avoid doodling.

Remember your stomach!

Don't eat a big meal before a meeting. Less obviously, avoid chocolate and other fatty sweets. Your body gets a 'chocolate boost' but that is quickly followed by a slump as the sugar is cleaned out of your bloodstream. In addition heavy fats like this take a lot of your body's energy to digest, and most minute-takers would prefer that energy in their brain.

Use a break

If there is a short coffee break and you are getting tired, try to get moving – get the heart rate up a bit. Just walk swiftly up some stairs or along a corridor and back again.

Contributing minute-taker

It is difficult, if not impossible, to minute a meeting and contribute properly to it. Writing and talking are not activities that can be done at the same time. On the other hand, if you are a contributor to the meeting you are likely to have a higher level of knowledge of the subject. You also have the advantage of the status of group member, which makes it easier to interrupt and ask for help or information.

When taking notes you should not be writing down everything that is said by each individual. It is the topics discussed and the points raised that are of concern. You should not therefore need to write down what everyone is saying.

If you contribute to one item

Before the meeting, ask another member of the group to take minutes during your item. Try to remind the member of this before the item starts.

If you contribute throughout

It is simply not possible to take detailed notes and contribute. The group have to accept shorter (but no less accurate) minutes and an action point. You can reduce your notes accordingly. If this is not acceptable to the group, use 'Committee business' to schedule a discussion on how the meeting is run, present it as a problem and let everyone decide what should be done.

Since you have the status of contributor, if the chairperson does not summarise at the end of each item, you can interrupt and do so. Usually this is done by saying 'Excuse me, can I confirm for the minutes...?' You can even tape this, using a dictating machine, and you have the basis for your minutes. If the chairperson does summarise, this too can be taped (with agreement), but do not try to tape the whole meeting.

8

Taking notes

One of the greatest areas of concern for minute-takers is recoginising what should be noted and sifting out the irrelevant information. This is known as ignoring the drivel and picking out the pearl!

Before you start to take notes, it is important to get the 'mechanics' correct. Handwriting, as such, is seldom taught in schools and as a result we fall prey to bad habits that leave us walking out of the meeting with a stiff arm, sore shoulder and often an unnecessary headache.

The mechanics of writing

- *Sit properly*
 Sit back and 'square' in your chair so that your back and legs are supported.
- *Find a good pen or pencil*
 Ignore all the advice that pen is better, or pencil is what the experts use. You will write more quickly and legibly with the instrument that you like best. Experiment and then make sure you always take at least two into the

meeting. Try to find one that has a rubber or ridged grip so that your hand does not slip, and that is not so narrow that your hand is pinched in holding it. Some people find it useful to take red or green pens to highlight actions or make other notes. If you can manage this and use the right colour at the right time, then it may be worth trying. Otherwise, use symbols or the layout of your notes to differentiate.

- *Support your arm below your elbow*
 Don't take your arm's weight on the wrist; after all, it's the joint that you need to move in order to write. Move in towards the table, so that the weight of your arm is taken just below your elbow. This frees your lower arm to move and will significantly reduce the arm and shoulder ache.
- *Use your non-writing hand to manage the paper*
 Don't leave the paper stationary and move your writing hand forward and back. Rather, keep your writing arm static (see the next section) and move the paper away from you as you work down the page.
- *If you don't have the 'luxury' of a table*
 Take a good quality clipboard so that the paper is well supported. Use a chair with arms and support your writing arm as above, moving the paper with the clipboard towards and away from you as you write.
- *Use A4 paper*
 Use good-quality paper so that the pen glides over it without catching. Make sure you have a right and left margin and then draw a further vertical line about three-quarters of the way across the page. This will leave you with the approximate width of a shorthand pad. You should use the wider column for taking notes and the narrower one for necessary arrows, asterisks, cross-references, etc.

 The left margin can be used for noting the initials of each speaker, the right for the initials of someone responsible for an action point. See Figure 8.1.

Initials of speakers	Notes	Extra space for arrows, extra notes, etc.	Initials of action takers

Figure 8.1 Paper ruled for structured note taking

See also Figure 8.5 for an example with notes. You might find it helpful to use a spiral-bound pad to help keep the sheets in order.

- *Take notes on an 'extended' agenda*
 A contradictory idea that might suit you is to print off a copy of the agenda with extra space between the headings and make your notes on this.

Taking notes

Use bullet points, not sentences

If you write full sentences, you are likely to take down all the unnecessary 'filling in' words, often scribbling down the words that people say (see Figure 8.2). Not only will you have much that

Open at Christmas?

Always closed between Christmas Eve and January 3.

Everyone's closed, our customers and competitors.

Complaints last year from customers who were working.

We could pick up sales – But how many buy?

It'll be quiet – always is – can catch up on paperwork. Several staff happy to work – We'll have to pay overtime – no, not necessary. It's working days, not bank hols.

How could we decide who's working. The department could do it themselves. What if no-one wants to work in a department? Not all need to be open. Which do? Sales and any others that want to.

Many customers now are small businesses – we could pick up some orders as they'll be working. Stores need to be open – no point selling if can't deliver. So Sales and Stores to be asked to provide rota for staying open – skeleton staff. Others can work if want to.

Figure 8.2 Don't write essay-style notes

is not needed, but it will be harder to make sense of the notes, which will look like a school essay.

Write bullet points, working down the page, not across it (see Figure 8.3). If you write across the page, you are more likely to put in the 'padding' words and you will end up scribbling furiously as described above. Figure 8.4 shows an example of working bullet points down the page, and Figure 8.5 of bullet points on paper ruled for structured note taking.

Open at Christmas?

Some customers complained. Could pick up sales – not many, can catch up on paperwork. Staff happy to work. Pay overtime? – no

Who to work? Departments sort themselves. What if no-one wants to? Not all need to open, sales do + any others, pick up some orders as customers working

Stores open – must deliver sales

Sales and stores provide rota – skeleton staff, others can work if want to.

Figure 8.3 Don't write bullet points across the page

Taping a meeting

Although taping a meeting might sound appealing in theory, the reality is seldom successful. The most common problems are:

- **the machine picking up all the extraneous noises such as shuffling papers, removing glasses, pouring water;**
- **difficulty in recognising voices;**
- **managing the machine, turning tapes, etc;**
- **risk of the machine not taping;**
- **participants' discomfort with being taped;**
- **boredom listening to it a second time around.**

Using a dictating machine to summarise

If you are a participant in the meeting as well as the minute-taker, you do have the advantage of a greater status within the group. If the chairperson summarises, this can be taped (with permission). However, if this does not happen, interrupt as each

item closes and summarise the discussion, checking with the others that you are correct. If you tape this, you will have the basis of your minutes.

Using a laptop

Unlike taping the meeting, using a laptop does have some advantages: 1) the notes are already on the computer; and 2) it's quicker to type than to write. However, there are also disadvantages:

Open at Christmas?

Some customers complained

Could pick up sales – not many

can catch up on paperwork

staff happy to work

pay overtime? – no

who to work?

departments sort themselves

What if no one wants to

Not all need to open

Sales do

+ any others

pick up some orders and customers working

stores open – must deliver sales

sales and stores provide rota – skeleton staff

Others can work if want to

Figure 8.4 Take bullet points, working down the page, with plenty of white space

- You can only add to the end of the document. Whilst it is possible in theory to scroll through, in reality trying to find your place as you move through the document is difficult.
- Participants are often fascinated by watching a typist type, which is off-putting.
- The sound can be a distraction.

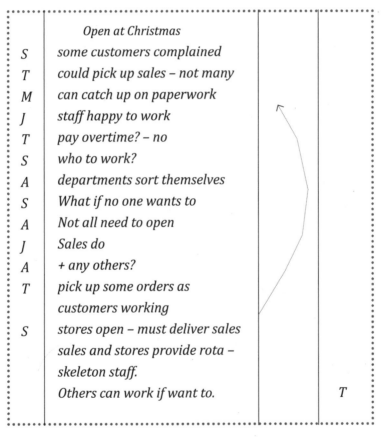

	Open at Christmas
S	*some customers complained*
T	*could pick up sales – not many*
M	*can catch up on paperwork*
J	*staff happy to work*
T	*pay overtime? – no*
S	*who to work?*
A	*departments sort themselves*
S	*What if no one wants to*
A	*Not all need to open*
J	*Sales do*
A	*+ any others?*
T	*pick up some orders as*
	customers working
S	*stores open – must deliver sales*
	sales and stores provide rota –
	skeleton staff.
	Others can work if want to.

Figure 8.5 Bullet points with notes, using the column for arrows, etc

Look as well as listen

Although you will usually be looking at what you are writing, it is
important to remember eye contact:

- *Eye contact improves your hearing*
 It is easier to hear what someone is saying if you are
 watching as well as listening.
- *Eye contact reminds speakers of your presence*
 If you catch eye contact with speakers, they are
 reminded of your presence and are more likely to
 include you in their 'audience', which again makes it
 easier to hear.
- *Achieving eye contact*
 Although you need to look at what you are writing,
 when you hear the voice change, glance up and look
 properly at the new speaker, if possible catching his or
 her eye to demonstrate that you are listening. If you
 recognise that you have already noted a point, stop, look
 and listen, if necessary nodding encouragingly (a small
 movement!).

The message, not the words

The key skill that a minute-taker needs is the ability to record the
message, not the words. When someone is speaking, words come
from the mouth, but the message comes from the brain. For
example, the following people are all saying broadly the same
thing (extracts from a discussion on the possibility of staying
open over the Christmas holiday) – it is only the first one who
ties up mouth and brain.

- **'Staying open between Christmas and New Year is worth
 considering seriously.'**

- 'When I worked for Amercall, we always opened between Christmas and New Year and often picked up orders from competitors who were closed.'
- 'Quite a few staff are happy to work over the holiday period and take leave later in the year.'
- 'Several customers commented that they could not reach us during the Christmas fortnight.'
- 'Last year we lost several orders by not answering calls in the sales office over the holiday period.'
- 'Even if sales are quiet, it is one of the few times when we can catch up with the paperwork, reorganise systems and so on.'
- 'When I worked with the sales team, I used to hate the aftermath of the Christmas holiday. January low spirits combined with a rush of business, and the office was in chaos from a long shutdown after a chaotic Christmas party season. We always started the year with a backlog.'

Beware voice tone/delivery

Another aspect of listening for the message, not the words, is to take note of voice tone and delivery but not to be swept along by them. For example, try saying the following sentence in a variety of tones, staged from neutral through to furious (you might want to add a few extra words): 'Most of the team don't know how to work the receiver.'

No matter how the words are said, the message remains the same. Have a look at the example quotes in the box, together with how they appeared informally in the minute-taker's notes.

'All the furniture in this office is old; it's scruffy and much of it is falling apart. We should do something about replacing it. It looks dreadful and one day there's going to be an accident.'

The Office furniture needs replacing

'The phones must be answered by a human between 9.00 and 5.30; voicemail is only acceptable outside working hours. People don't like leaving a message and it gives the impression that we're keeping them at arm's length.'

Voicemail outside office hours only

'The goldfish have been a great success; many people commented that they were relaxing. It seemed to stop small children running around – they were more interested in watching the fish.'

goldfish – a good thing

'The clinic has seen a 30 per cent increase in patient throughput. It's not surprising that the car park gets full. Sometimes there's a queue back out on to the road. There's going to be an accident one day.'

The car park isn't big enough

'King Arthur had a point! The shape of the table is vital to the success of the meeting – I think we should consider a round table, or at least a broad oval. These long boardroom tables make sensible discussion impossible. I can't hear Ken and they're chatting at the back.'

Change shape of table to round/broad oval

'I used to work for a hospital in the Midlands, luckily not one of those in Birmingham city centre because parking is a non-starter. All the furniture there was incredibly old, probably from the 50s or even before. But it was strong and solid and outlasted all the newer 'cheap' stuff. Quality has to be a prime concern because it's cheaper in the long run.'

Must buy good quality –
long-term saving

'Staff don't know how to use the programs or the system. Computer training was offered to all staff in 2006, and 50 courses were run. In 2007 it was 45, in 2004 in was just 20, and in 2009 it was 9, but new programs are coming in all the time and we expect them to learn by magic.'

Need to provide computer training

'Everyone in this team wants the new system; well, a couple of the administrators aren't too keen but they'll come around. Oh, and Tim is anti – but he always is. Everyone else is keen.'

Views are mixed about new system

Developing the skill

As we've seen, the essential skill is not the ability to write fast, but the ability to recognise what someone is talking about and identify the message. There are many everyday opportunities to develop this skill:

- **Alone, for example in the car, listen to the news headlines and at the same time say aloud what they are about:**

- inflation figures;
- riots in the Middle East;
- bed shortages in the health service;
- England's cricket victory;
- bus crash;
- football violence.
- As soon as you are confident of these, take it a stage forward and add in the crucial message:
 - inflation figures, up by 3 per cent;
 - riots in the Middle East, two deaths and many injured;
 - bed shortages in the health service, worries about A & E patients left on trolleys;
 - England's cricket victory, by eight runs with three overs to play;
 - bus crash, no-one injured;
 - football violence, many arrests.
- Watch television drama or soap operas and, as you watch the scene, define what it is about and the key arguments: 'They're arguing about where to live: he wants to stay with his parents; she wants them to get their own flat.'
- Watch celebrity or sports interviews and do the same thing: 'He played football as a child; he was spotted by a sports coach at his local club.'
- Summarise back or 'reflect' what has been said to you: 'So when the machine didn't work you checked for paper jam, the paper stock and the toner cartridge.'
- Mentally summarise conversations around you: 'She enjoyed the group charter of a boat; he didn't – wasn't with a friendly group.'

9

Structuring notes

Even with the best chairperson and a well-disciplined committee, you are likely to find that the discussion jumps around within an agenda item. For most minute-takers, making sense of a discussion with many different aspects is a significant problem. Some of the time you can move around your notes as you take them and add information where it is relevant. On other occasions, your notes will follow the order of the discussion and need to be structured at the writing-up stage.

Follow the agenda

Whatever numbering and headings appear on the agenda must also appear in the minutes.

If the meeting used a 'basic' agenda

If the agenda was very general, the minute-taker will have to take each subject within the agenda item and write it up, presenting the information grouped and in a logical order.

For example, if the committee discussed 'redecoration of canteen', their concerns will range through the amount of money

to be spent; the colour scheme to be chosen; whether to replace furniture and, if so, with what; the lighting and so on. They are unlikely to deal with each and move on; rather it will be discussion that touches repeatedly on the different points. Actions will come as and when decided and will often be revisited and changed.

In the minutes, the discussion on 'redecoration of canteen' is likely to be divided into several subheadings, which can be done without affecting the continuity between the agenda and minute numbering.

If the meeting used a full or objectives agenda

By breaking up the discussion into smaller sections, the discussion becomes more structured, but even so, there will be different aspects to consider.

For example, one subsection of the discussion on redecorating the canteen was 'furniture'. Within that, the committee will discuss tables and chairs. The discussion on tables is likely to cover colour, material, shape, size. Again, the numbering and headings on the agenda are likely to be subdivided, either into headings or simply by using paragraphs (whichever is most appropriate).

It is quite possible to type up the notes, delete duplication and 'cut and paste' them to achieve a logical order. However, this is a time-consuming process and it is much faster to decide on the structure before writing. That way you only write up the notes that you need.

During the discussion a participant might raise an aspect of the discussion that is relevant to the subject, but not listed on the agenda. For example, your agenda might show the item in Figure 9.1.

If at any time during the discussion on these points the subject of flooring is raised and discussed, it must be minuted because it is relevant. Wherever it is discussed, use the next free number within the main agenda item to minute it (see Figure 9.2).

7. Redecoration of canteen
 7.1 Budget
 7.2 Colour scheme
 7.3 Furniture
 7.4 Lights

Figure 9.1 Extract from a full agenda

7. **Redecoration of canteen**
 7.1 Budget
 In comparison with the rest of the fifth-floor renovation, the cost of the canteen redecoration...
 7.2 Colour scheme
 The canteen is a light room and therefore...
 7.3 Furniture
 The furniture must be in keeping with the general style and colour of the canteen and...
 7.4 Lights
 Several staff have complained about the strip lights causing headaches...
 7.5 Flooring
 The current flooring is in good condition and is a neutral colour...

Figure 9.2 Add the new item at the end of the planned and numbered items

If the subject is not on the agenda at all

Provided the item is relevant to the work of the group it should be minuted. If there is not a section where it can slot in, include it under 'Any other business'.

Not many people making suggestions
Only 4 last month
Why? system is stale
* no reason to make the effort*
* no one wants to be the only 'goody goody' who*
* suggests*
Give up on it? Run for six years.
Or encourage use – how?
* write-up in magazine*
* an award – certificate*
* financial reward*
* a gift*
Money is the key
How much? £5 – £50 – £20 – £50
For suggestions that are implemented
Who pays? – whoever benefits
Advertise the change? – noticeboards, e-mail
When/how to give: party
* by MD*
* by manager*
* internal post*
Arrange with manager, can present it or just hand it over.
Lots of money – too much?
If not a £50 saving, then idea won't be implemented
– must be an incentive

Figure 9.3 Notes taken during a discussion on the future of the suggestion scheme

Structuring your notes

Within an agenda item, the discussion is likely to jump around as individuals reintroduce their personal concerns or views. As minute-taker, you should ignore the order of the discussion and instead structure the minutes according to the order of the content.

Read through the notes in Figure 9.3, taken during an item on how to generate interest in the organisation's suggestion scheme.

These notes are broadly in the order of:

- **loss of interest;**
- **why it's happened;**
- **motivating staff to suggest;**
- **money;**
- **how to advertise the new system;**
- **how to hand over the reward;**
- **money/motivating staff to suggest;**
- **advertising the new system.**

As you can see there is some duplication. The most common way of dealing with this is to type up the notes and then start editing. To save time and improve the quality of the minutes, structure the notes before typing them up. Look at a suggested structure for the notes above (Figure 9.4).

Some minute-takers could produce the structure in Figure 9.4 in the meeting. Most would take notes as in Figure 9.3, then sort out the structure back in the office.

This structure has taken all the notes that could be used – a very detailed minute. If this was what was required, it could be written up as shown in the following box.

> The committee discussed the drop in support for the suggestion scheme. There was support for the system in principle and it was agreed that efforts should be made to generate more interest.
>
> In order to encourage suggestions, it was decided to offer a financial reward for successful ideas, and agreed that £50 was an appropriate figure. This will come from whichever budget benefits from the saving.
>
> The manager of successful staff members could arrange a presentation or simply pass the money on as deemed appropriate. In addition, the managing director would be informed so that a congratulatory note could be sent, and the idea would appear in the magazine.
>
> Staff should be informed of the changes through the newsletter and posters on the noticeboards.
> Suggestions made after 31 May would be eligible for the payment.
>
> *Posters to be put up during w/c 18 May*
> *Article to be inserted in May issue of newsletter*
>
> *Action:* **Tom Brind**
> 30 April 2009

This minute is in the structure/order of: interest waning; how to motivate; how to give; telling staff.

For most purposes, only some of the information would be used to write a shorter minute. The structure would then look like the one in Figure 9.5.

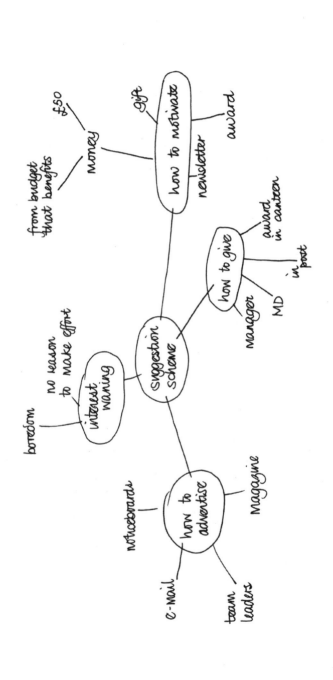

Figure 9.4 Discussion notes, structured into logical groups

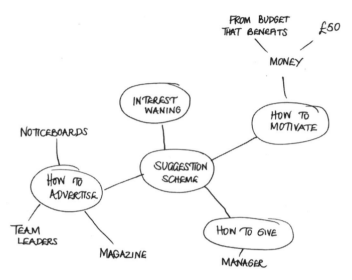

Figure 9.5 Structure for a briefer minute

A briefer minute would be written up as shown in the following box.

> **The committe discussed the drop in support for the suggestion scheme. It was decided to offer a £50 reward for successful ideas, to come from whichever budget benefits from the saving.**
>
> **The money will be given by the relevant manager. The managing director would be informed so that a congratulatory note could be sent, and the idea would appear in the magazine.**
>
> **Suggestions made after 31 May would be eligible for the payment.**
>
> *Posters to be put up during w/c 18 May*
> *Article to be instered in May issue of newsletter*
>
> Action: ***Tom Brind***
> 30 April 2009

Using the structure

To use a structure like the one outlined above, note your subject in the centre of the space. Take each point you have noted and decide whether it is relevant. If it is, look to see whether it relates to a point that you already have. If it does, link the two. If it does not, start a new 'area'. This process is illustrated in Figure 9.6.

Structuring your notes like this will mean that you have the skeleton of the minute before you write, which saves considerable time in writing and editing. Also, interruptions won't cause you to lose your train of thought, as they could do if you are 'translating' your notes into sentences. In addition, as you go through the process you generally move from the wording in your notes (words they may have said) to your phrasing (a summary of their message). Type the minutes from your structure, referring to your notes when you need more detail.

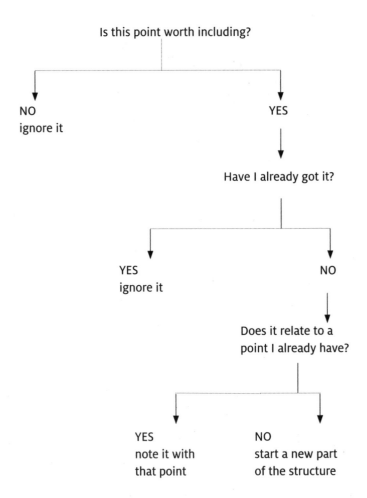

Figure 9.6 Process for structuring notes

10

Writing up the minutes

Minutes are not a record of what was said. They are a record of what was discussed.

In order to save time, write up the minutes quickly, certainly within a day. If they are to perform the function of reminding participants of their actions, they must be circulated within a week (within a couple of days for a weekly meeting).

The longer you put off the task, the more time-consuming and difficult it becomes. Your memory of the meeting will fade, as will the memory of anyone you might need to ask for help. This means the minutes will take longer to write and are likely to be less accurate. You will also waste time looking at your notes and then putting them back in the in-tray.

Speeding up the process

Prepare templates or master documents

For each meeting set up a master document with the heading, the list of those who can attend and so on. All you will then have to do is 'cut and paste' the names to the correct headings, copy across the main agenda headings and fill in the detail.

Inserting variable information

You can save time by setting up your master document with variable information (such as the date) replaced with a symbol: # is an easy one to choose because it is near the return key. Make sure that the # is in the format (size and highlighting) of the text that will replace it. Write a macro to find the # symbol (CTRL # is a simple one to use). This means that every time you type [CTRL #], the cursor will jump to the next # sign and highlight it. You just have to type in the information and it will replace the # with text in the right formatting.

Make sure that your formatting for the action column or any similar requirements are correct and you're ready to go. Just open the master document, save as a new document, copy across the main agenda headings and start typing. Figure 10.1 shows an example master document.

Start by looking back over the agenda to decide on the item which you understand most clearly. Turn to the minutes document and find the relevant heading. Define the action point (what is to be done, by whom and when); don't worry about perfect English at this stage but be accurate and precise. Now go through your notes for that item and delete notes you shouldn't have taken (usually irrelevance) and notes you have duplicated. For each note that remains, go through the structuring process outlined in Chapter 9 (see particularly Figure 9.5) and then type up that item. Repeat this process, inserting the text in the correct place in the document, and before you know it the minutes will be done.

Of course some people prefer to work from top to bottom, and if that suits you, then that should be your approach. The point about defining the action before the text still remains, though.

Name of Committee <center>#—#</center> <center>#</center>	# symbols formatted as heading to be used with macro to insert information for date, time and place	
Present Linda Curzon George Ellaway Nicola Goodenough Robert Hawthorne Sharon Kinning Elias Oswald Gerald Palin Patrick Pau	**Apologies** **Absent** **Copy**	All names listed, ready to be 'cut and pasted' to the appropriate heading in the minutes (usually laid out in a table)

In attendance

1. **Committee business**

 #

The # symbol is in the format of the text and will be replaced with type

2. **Minutes of the previous meeting**

 The minutes of the meeting held on # were # approved

3. **Matters arising**

Corrections should be inserted above this sentence.
The first # symbol will be replaced with the date and the second either deleted if there are no corrections or replaced with 'subsequently'

The agenda can be 'cut and pasted' from here and the detail filled in

Figure 10.1 Example master document, using the # symbol to pre-format text and mark insertion points

If you can't type the minutes for a few days

Spend a few minutes reading your notes at the end of the meeting

Avoid returning to your desk until you have spent five minutes or so reading your notes, editing and adding bits. Once you return to the phone messages and an overflowing in-tray, your memory will start to fade.

Use a dictating machine

You can go over your notes with a dictating machine. Do not try to dictate as though to a secretary, just add your verbal thoughts and comments to your written notes. The minutes can then be typed up from the mix of notes and audio.

Get the chairperson's approval

The chairperson is responsible for the minutes (even though you have done the work) and must approve them before dispatch. This serves as a double-check on what you have written.

Don't take amendments until the next meeting

Once you send out the minutes you might get corrections phoned or e-mailed to you. These can be noted, but the minutes should not be amended until the next meeting when everyone can be made aware of the amendments and have the opportunity to comment on them.

11

The minutes

Minutes, like all business writing, have changed in style over the years. As with letters and reports, the drive is towards plain English with short sentences and paragraphs, and a clear, reader-friendly style.

Minutes have also become shorter. In most cases 2 pages that are read are preferred to 10 pages that are filed. There are, however, still some conventions that are followed when writing them. Generally, these have survived because they are sensible, serving a practical purpose.

Heading

The heading of the minutes should follow the style of the agenda, whether that be the traditional paragraph style or the more modern centred layout (see Figures 11.1 and 11.2).

If you gave a predicted closing time on the agenda heading, give the actual time the meeting closed in the heading of the minutes. If you did not, you can still include the closing time in the heading or it can be done as a simple line at the end of the minutes (see 'close of meeting', below).

> Minutes of the IT User Group meeting held on 23 June 2009
> from 10.30 to 12.15 in meeting room 6, Emmerson House.

Figure 11.1 Example paragrph-style heading

> **IT User Group Meeting**
>
> 23 June 2009, 10.30–12.15
> Meeting room 6, Emmerson House
>
> **MINUTES**

Figure 11.2 Example centred layout heading

Who attended

The names at the start of a set of minutes are often thought of as 'who was there?' In fact the priority is 'who are the group?' They are simply arranged according to whether or not they attended, and in what capacity.

For a regular group, there are six headings that can be used. Few need all six but the order of those used should remain the same.

Present

The names of those who attended are shown in one or two columns at the start of the minutes. The chairperson is usually listed first with the others following in alphabetical order. Avoid any order of hierarchy, or differentiation like clinical/managerial or uniformed/civilian, as this highlights differences between the groups that are usually discouraged.

It is generally preferable to show the department or organisation represented. This is particularly useful when people move jobs frequently and it may be important to show the context in which they attended the meeting.

It should be enough to show first name and surname although you can include the title. If you do this be consistent: if you put Dr Adam Vernon, you must put Mr Victor Andrews.

For a one-off or general meeting, those who attended are generally listed under 'Attendees' or 'Attended'. This indicates a one-off meeting, whereas 'Present' is used to describe a core group.

In attendance

For those who are attending on a one-off basis, generally the name and department or organisation are shown. You can also choose to show when they attended. This is done by noting the item number after the name. If you do this, those with no number are assumed to have attended the whole meeting. An example is shown in Figure 11.3.

In attendance		
Desmond Barnham	Communications	
Sandy McPherson	J M Albany Ltd	item 9
Andy Morris	Secretariat	to item 6
Corinne Thorney	IT, Head Office	from item 3
Mel Wilson	Newman & Co.	items 4–8

Figure 11.3 Information that should be included under 'In attendance'

The minute-taker is listed under 'In attendance' with either 'minute-taker' or 'secretary' after the name. Although it is a minor difference, minute-taker implies that you took the notes and

typed them up, whereas secretary indicates that you organised the agenda, booked the room, etc.

The key difference between 'Present' and 'In attendance' comes historically from the days when decisions were proposed, seconded and voted upon. Those listed in 'Present' could vote and thus were responsible for the outcomes. This is why the minute-taker is listed in 'In Attendance' even though he or she is a member of the group.

Observer

Observers are those who are only there to watch. They may be internal staff, perhaps trainees or those with a specific interest in the subject. In the case of a public meeting, members of the public are listed here because they do not take an active part in the decision-making process. They do not have to be named, but can be listed as 'Members of the public (27)'. If there are reporters present they can be listed as either 'The press (3)' or with the publications detailed.

Substitutions

There are two ways to approach these. The first way is to list the substitute under 'In attendance' with the name of the original member in place of the department/organisation (see Figure 11.4). (This can also be done in 'Present' if you prefer.)

In attendance

Joseph Roberts	On behalf of Robert Hayford
Hayley Worth	IT Group
Tris Young	Infotec Logistics Ltd

Figure 11.4 Example style for listing a substitute

The second way is to list the original member in 'Present' but with 'represented by [name]' after the name (see Figure 11.5). This

is generally preferable because it is the original member who takes responsibility.

```
Present

John King                   Chair
Sue McEwan
Tom Mills
Rosham Patel
Robert Hayford              represented by Joseph Roberts
```

Figure 11.5 Alternative style for listing a substitute

Apologies

For a regular meeting or one where specific people have been invited, people who do not attend the meeting fall into two groups: 1) those who have apologised; and 2) those who do not turn up.

Apologies can be made:

- **when the date of the meeting is set during the previous meeting (nothing to put on that meeting's minutes; include under 'Apologies' on the minutes of the meeting that is missed);**
- **during the intervening period;**
- **on the day via a message from a colleague who is attending.**

These members are listed under 'Apologies'.

Anyone you expect, but who does not turn up, should be listed under 'Absent'. It is important not just to leave off the names of those who don't attend. You are providing a record of who attended a meeting and a broader record of who was

involved in that group at that time. Using 'Absent' gives you a complete list for administrative purposes and means the record is complete (and makes a comment about those whose commitment is questionable).

Although the heading 'Apologies' is used on the agenda, the names are often included in a list at the start of the minutes, after those who are present (see Figure 11.6). If you plan to do this, do not number 'Apologies' on the agenda or your numbering will be one place awry.

Present			In attendance	
Helen Pratt	Finance	(chair)	Frank Moss	Security item 8
Mark Delby	Marketing		Tina Parker	Minute-taker
Marion Fowkes	Finance			
Susannah Lewis	Sales		**Apologies**	
Roger Oswald	Marketing		Sulima Begum	Administration
Brian Winner	Finance			
Nick Wordsley	Administration		**Absent**	
Lizzie Young	Sales		Mary King	Sales

Figure 11.6 Example layout for including 'Apologies' as part of the listing at the top of the minutes

If you would rather number 'Apologies' on the agenda, start your minutes with this as the first item and include the names as two separate sentences (or paragraphs, if necessary), one for 'Apologies' and one for 'Absent' (see Figure 11.7).

> 1. **Apologies**
> Apologies were received from Sulima Begum, Anthony Edler and Clive Roberts. Mary King and Robin Lyle were absent.

Figure 11.7 Example of layout including 'Apologies' as part of the text

For a meeting that is open to a wide group of people, for example all nursing staff within the hospital, only note those who have apologised. The others can be left off.

Copy

If the minutes are circulated to any individual or group other than those involved in the meeting (and listed above), they should be detailed in this section. This might mean giving names or general groups (eg 'All team leaders') or perhaps the most general of all, 'Noticeboards'. Other headings for this could be 'For information', 'Circulation', 'Distribution', or similar.

Introduction

It is unusual to see any introduction in the minutes. It is usually general, just the chairperson getting the meeting off to a businesslike start, and therefore need not be mentioned. If it is planned to use this as a more significant section, it should be on the agenda and should be minuted. If there is no intention to minute it, but something relevant is said that cannot go elsewhere, start the minutes with a paragraph to cover it, using no numbering or heading. That way the numbering and headings will remain correct.

Declarations of interest

Note any that are made, being consistent over whether the reason is given. What happened as a result should also be noted, showing that the person either did not contribute to the discussion or left the meeting.

Committee business

Any items raised under 'Committee business' should be minuted in the same style and layout as main agenda items.

Minutes of the previous meeting

It is important to confirm that the minutes of the previous meeting were accepted, or that the group wanted particular changes.

If the minutes are correct

There are a number of variations that are acceptable:

- **The minutes of the meeting held on [date] were approved.**
- **The minutes of the meeting held on [date] were accepted.**
- **The minutes of the meeting held on [date] were accepted as an accurate record.**
- **The minutes of the meeting held on [date] were signed.**

If you have given the date of the last meeting in the heading ('Minutes of the meeting held on [date]') the wording shown will change to 'The minutes of the previous meeting were...'

If there are errors

You can use a subheading of 'Amendments' and put any changes after this, or merely start with the first heading that contained an error (see Figure 11.8). Avoid putting 'changed from... to...' as this tends to muddle the reader. When all changes have been noted, type 'The minutes of the meeting held on [date] were subsequently approved...'

Don't send out a corrected set of minutes – most people file both or the wrong one! Make sure that the file copy shows both

how the minutes were circulated and the corrections. This can be done by:

- leaving handwritten corrections on the set of minutes;
- correcting the minutes from the last meeting but attaching a copy of 'Minutes of the previous meeting' to the current one so that the changes can be seen;
- not correcting the minutes from the last meeting, but just attaching a copy of 'Minutes of the previous meeting', again, so changes can be seen.

3.0 **Minutes of the previous meeting**

3.1 **Car park**
The islands will be raised 10 cm above ground level.

3.2 **Reception flooring**
Second sentence to be replaced with:
The flooring would not have an obvious pattern such as the current design incorporating the logo. A muted pattern that allows the appearance of solid colour would be advisable to reduce the appearance of dirt.

3.3 **Renovation of storage sheds**
The deadline for completion of the renovation is December 2009.

The minutes of the meeting held on [date] were subsequently approved.

Figure 11.8 Example layout for correcting previous minutes

Signing minutes

Minutes are signed as extra proof that everyone at the table agreed to their accuracy. Although seldom done these days, it is worth considering in case of future dispute. The chairperson should sign them on the front cover or last page, and every other page should be initialled. The minutes of the meeting will say

that the 'Minutes of the meeting held on [date] were signed as an accurate record.'

Matters arising

As discussed earlier, 'Matters arising' is often taken up with participants arguing over something already decided in a previous meeting or by individuals going into great detail of *how* they completed the action. Neither is required for the minutes.

Text is acceptable under 'Matters arising', but only when it is worthy of inclusion in its own right: for example, when an aspect of an action point needs consideration but was not discussed during the original meeting. Most of the time you should minute the true purpose of 'Matters arising' – to confirm that actions that were agreed have been taken.

This can be done as a table, or certainly with the minimum of text (see Figure 11.9).

4. **Matters arising**

4.1	Car park barrier (3.4/03.09*)	Completed	
4.2	Publicity for David Smith's visit (5.2)	In hand	
4.3	Outdoor smoking area (6) It was agreed to leave the area for storage for six months before decoration	In hand	**H Wheatley** 27 November 2009
4.4	Canteen chairs (7.2)	No action taken due to merger	
4.5	Delivery standards (8.2)		**D Simmonds** 28 August 2006

*indicates item 3.4 from the meeting held in March 2009. If no meeting date is given, the item is assumed to come from the previous meeting.

Figure 11.9 Example table layout for 'Matters arising'

The five options in the 'status' column in Figure 11.9 are examples of the options available to you when minuting matters arising:

- *Completed* (if the action is finished)
 This indicates that the action has been completed in the form, and to the stage, detailed in the earlier minutes. The matter is now closed.
- *In hand* (if the action is very near completion)
 If there is nothing else shown, 'in hand' indicates that the action is so near completion that it is as good as done. The group have assumed that it will be completed, and the matter is closed with no further report-back required.
- *In hand plus a deadline and name/initials* (if the action is under way, but not near completion)
 If the person responsible has done little and a further report to confirm completion is required, again put 'in hand' but include a new deadline and name/initials in the action column. This will trigger it as a 'matter arising' at the agreed date. There is no need to state what action has been taken unless it is worthy of minuting.
- *A new deadline date* (where nothing has been done)
 If an action has been forgotten, just put a new deadline date and the initials of the person responsible so that it will come up again at a future meeting. You can restate the action point if you wish.
- *A reason for lack of action* (where nothing has been done for a good reason)
 If there is a good reason for not taking action, this should be given.

If you do not like the 'form' style of 'Matters arising', it can be done as text (see Figure 11.10), but make sure that you do not fall into the trap of minuting old argument or boring feedback. Just because something is said, that does not mean it should appear in the minutes!

4. Matters arising

 4.1 **Car park barrier** (3.4/03.06)
 The car park barrier has been repaired and painted, using
 reflective paint.

 4.2 **Publicity for David Smith's visit** (5.2)
 The press releases have been sent to all local papers.
 Publication is not expected until the week of the visit.

 4.3 **Outdoor smoking area** (6)
 Because of the lack of people using the area in favour of the
 car park, it was agreed to clean the area and then leave it for
 storage for six months before decoration.

 H Wheatley
 27 November 2009

 4.5 **Canteen chairs** (7.2)
 No action taken due to announcement of merger and
 uncertainty about the future of the site.

 4.6 **Delivery standards** (8.2)
 Meeting with post room to be **D Simmonds**
 arranged to confirm standards*. 28 August 2009

*this will repeat the action point from the earlier minutes

Figure 11.10 Example layout for 'Matters arising', giving minimal text

By using an agenda with the actions listed and these options in the minutes, every action that is agreed will be checked up on, confirmed or if necessary taken forward in a managed way, and this is recorded in the minutes.

Where the whole meeting is matters arising

A whole meeting can be matters arising, usually for project-planning types of meetings. The minutes for these are likely to be in sections that relate to the project (see Figure 11.11), and each participant will confirm actions and raise current concerns.

These concerns will be discussed and new actions may arise. If this is the case, for each heading start with the relevant actions and confirm their status before moving on to new discussion.

Reports

Reports are the items that are to be received only – not for discussion. A report that precedes a discussion will be dealt with as a main agenda item, but the guidelines for minuting it are the same.

11. **Launch Party**

 Guest List
 The guest list has been drawn up and invitations sent.
 Press coverage
 Invitations have been sent to local papers and trade press.

 11.1 **Invitations to staff from other offices**
 The committee discussed extending invitations to senior management from all regional offices. In the interests of maximising communications throughout the group, it was suggested that seniority was not a factor and that although one senior manager should be invited, a number of other invitations should be sent to each office.

 It was agreed to invite each regional manager and two other staff from each office. A letter to the manager to suggest colleagues from different departments would be preferred.

 Ceri Jones
 30 October 2009

Figure 11.11 Example matters arising incorporated in minutes for a meeting that is entirely 'Matters arising'

Reports should always be circulated in writing with the agenda so that participants can read them beforehand. It is not only the minute-taker who will struggle with a report – only those with a good understanding of the subject will be able to follow, and many participants just switch off.

Where the report is circulated with the agenda

There is no need to summarise what is said, as everyone will have a copy. It can be worded along the lines of:

- **The committee received the finance director's report.**
- **The committee received the finance report.**
- **The finance director gave a report on the third quarter.**

Where the report is tabled (given out on the day)

The minutes should read as above. A copy can be attached for non-attenders or, to save paper, simply add, 'Copy/information available from...'

Where the report is verbal

Unless you have excellent shorthand there is not much chance of keeping up with reports because they tend to be fast and factual, often delivered in the rather flat style of reading aloud. You should either: ask the person to give you a copy and attach it to the minutes; or ask the person to give you a few-line summary for the minutes.

If you have to note the report

If there is no option but to minute the report, cover only the briefest detail, usually what was talked about. For example, the minutes of a 10-minute report are shown in the following box.

> The team received a report on the experimental use of temporary sales staff, detailing the cost of the programme (£8,400), the benefits of short-term staff and the problems that resulted. The use of temporary staff will not be continued.

Main agenda items

Minutes must follow the order, numbering and headings of the agenda, but extra headings can be used providing the numbering remains the same. See Chapter 9 on structuring notes for more information.

The style of minutes has changed, and continues to do so. Along with the drive towards shorter, plain English writing has come a preference for a slightly less formal style. That is not the same as saying that minutes should be casual. The writing is still businesslike, but many minute-takers prefer to focus on what is being discussed (factual minutes) rather than on what the committee did (traditional style). Both styles are 'correct'; the choice should be based on the preference of the chairperson and the committee (and, of course, the minute-taker).

Traditional style

Traditional minutes report what the committee did (see Figure 11.12). They are written in the past tense, looking back to what happened at the meeting. The phrasing depends on what happened. Consider these examples:

- **The Training Manager explained that the second 'Investors in People' visit had been postponed.**
- **It was reported that the second 'Investors in People' visit had been postponed.**

- The committee heard that the second 'Investors in People' visit had been postponed.
- The committee discussed the postponement of the second 'Investors in People' visit.
- It was suggested that the commitment to 'Investors in People' may be weakening.
- The committee agreed that the commitment to 'Investors in People' was as strong as ever.

Factual style

Factual minutes report on the situation as it was discussed (see Figure 11.13). They are written in the appropriate tense and, again, the phrasing depends on what was discussed. Consider these examples:

- The second 'Investors in People' visit has been postponed.
- Commitment to 'Investors in People' may be weakening.
- Commitment to 'Investors in People' is as strong as ever.

The commitee discussed the possibility of a branch falling on the temporary building. It was suggested that the building should not be sited so near the boundary, but no other location could be found. It was agreed to ask a tree surgeon to advise on the state of the trees and then discuss the location in the light of his comments.

Advice on condition of trees and risk to building to be discussed with Ark Woodland Care **Nigel Hamlyn**
16 October 2009

Figure 11.12 Example minute in traditional style

Any other business

Items taken under 'Any other business' should be minuted in the same style and format as the main agenda items. Give each a

number and subheading under the main heading of 'Any other business'.

> There is a possibility of a branch falling on the temporary building. As no other location can be found, a tree surgeon will be asked to advise on the state of the trees. The location can then be discussed.
> *Advice on condition of trees and risk to building*
> *to be discussed with Ark Woodland Care* **Nigel Hamlyn**
> 16 October 2009

Figure 11.13 Example minute in factual style

Beware irrelevant items

People will often take the chance of a captive audience to give out information or discuss things that are relevant to the individuals concerned, but not to the reason they are meeting at that time; in other words, issues that are outside the terms of reference or objective for the group. These should not form part of the minutes. If it is necessary to circulate the information, it should be done as a separate note.

Items deferred to next meeting

Where the group do not have the time or necessary information to discuss an item, it will usually be put on the agenda for the next meeting. If this is a one-off, just minute the heading and note that it was deferred. If there are several items, you can use a heading of 'Items deferred to next meeting' and list them.

Items referred to another group

This should be dealt with in the same way as items deferred to the next meeting.

Date of next meeting

The date, time and place of the next meeting should be noted. If the meetings are set some time in advance, list the next few meetings.

It is also helpful to give a deadline for the receipt of agenda items (usually about eight days before the meeting) and a contact name and phone number/e-mail for agenda items, apologies, etc (see Figure 11.14).

Date of next meeting

The next meeting will be held at 11.15 am on 23 June 2009 in Room 7. Agenda items to be received by 12 June (Sue Thomas, x–2458, sue.thomas@marshalls.co.uk).

Figure 11.14 Example wording for 'Date of next meeting'

Close of meeting

If you have not shown the closing time as part of the heading, close the minutes with 'The meeting closed at [time].'

Styles of minutes

Summary

Summary minutes take the information that is to be given and present it in a logical order according to the content. Whilst the overall structure of headings and numbering must appear as it is in the agenda, the order of information within each agenda item is at the discretion of the minute-taker. See Chapter 9 for information on structuring.

Level of detail in summary minutes

There is no standard level of detail in minutes. Some groups want only the minimum detail and the outcome: basically a sentence or paragraph that justifies the action. Others want more information up to the point where minutes are very detailed indeed. Examples of summary minutes are given in Figures 11.15, 11.16 and 11.17.

Staffing of NTB clinic

A minimum of three nurses and a full-time secretary/receptionist will be required for each clinic session. The nursing posts can be flexible but applicants will have to commit themselves to certain clinics each week and cover for holidays and sickness.

Draft advertisements to be cleared with Personnel and placed on noticeboards and on 'e-jobs4U'

Rashiv Seduin (5/10/09)

Figure 11.15 Example of brief summary minute

Verbatim

In the context of minutes, verbatim does not mean word for word, but rather that the minutes follow the path of the discussion. With a good chairperson and disciplined committee, this may well be no problem. However, a more typical group will keep returning to certain aspects of the discussion or may discuss those aspects in an order that is random.

For example, in discussing the purchase of a new table for the boardroom, the group may discuss budget, shape, size, colour and flexibility. They are unlikely to discuss each and then move on. Rather, each speaker will draw the discussion to the aspect that concerns him or her most, often returning to that particular point.

Staffing of NTB clinic
A minimum of three nurses will be required for each clinic session together with a secretary/receptionist.

As the clinic times will fall within normal working hours the administrative post will be full-time. Holiday/sickness cover can be arranged through the other health centre staff.

In order to be as 'family friendly' as possible, the nursing posts can be flexible, either three 30-hour/week posts or as many part-timers as needed to cover the shifts. Applicants will have to agree which clinics they want to cover and commit themselves to those periods. This means that the same nurse will run a particular clinic each week, leading to continuity for the patients. The nurses can increase hours to cover holiday and sickness periods, and for this reason part-time staff are preferable.

Draft advertisements to be cleared with Personnel and placed on noticeboards and on 'e-jobs4U'
Rashiv Seduin
(5/10/09)

Figure 11.16 Example of detailed summary minute (factual in style)

Verbatim minutes either follow the path of the discussion precisely, or, more commonly, take the order in which the aspects are raised and then group the information in that order. The overall structure will probably then be working downwards from the concerns of the person with the loudest voice.

Verbatim minutes tend to be long and boring, and few groups want them. An example is shown in Figure 11.18.

Action

Action minutes are hardly minutes at all. They are simply the agenda with the outcome of each discussion given after the headings (see Figure 11.19). If any text is required, the style is a brief summary.

Staffing of NTB clinic

The team discussed staffing of the new clinic. A minimum of three nurses would be required for each clinic session together with a secretary/receptionist.

As the clinic times would fall within normal working hours the administrative post would be full-time. Holiday/sickness cover could be arranged through the other heath centre staff.

In order to be as 'family friendly' as possible, the nursing posts could be flexible. It was agreed that there would be three 30-hour/week posts or as many part-timers as could cover the shifts. Applicants would have to agree which clinics they wished to cover and commit themselves to those periods. This would mean the same nurse would run a particular clinic each week, leading to continuity for the patients. It was hoped that the nurses would be able to increase hours to cover holiday and sickness periods, and for this reason part-time staff were preferred.

It was agreed that draft advertisements would be cleared with Personnel and placed on noticeboards and on 'e-jobs4U'
Rashiv Seduin (5/10/09)

Figure 11.17 Example of detailed summary minute (traditional in style)

Common questions about minutes
Do I include historical or background information?

At the start of a discussion, someone may begin by explaining the history of an issue. Quite often this is uninvited and, although relevant to the subject, is not necessarily of great interest. This should not be minuted. However, if that information is given because a large part of the group are not aware of it and need to know in order to discuss the subject, it can be minuted if you wish. Make sure it is a separate paragraph so that those who know already can easily skip it.

Staffing of NTB clinic

The committee discussed the issue of staffing for the new clinic and agreed that a minimum of three nurses would be required for each session. It was suggested that a full-time secretary/receptionist would also be needed.

There was concern that the unit should be seen to be as 'family friendly' as possible and that the nursing posts should be flexible.

The workload and possibility of a 25-hour/week administrative post were discussed at length. Periods of holiday/sickness could be covered by the other health centre staff. Because of the workload, it was decided that a full-time post was required.

Three 30-hour/week nursing posts or as many part-timers as could cover the shifts could be arranged. Applicants would have to agree which clinics they wished to cover and commit themselves to those periods. This would mean the same nurse would run a particular clinic each week, leading to continuity for the patients. Concerns were expressed about holiday and sickness periods and it was agreed that part-time staff would be preferred as hours could be changed/increased to provide cover.

Draft advertisements to be cleared with Personnel and placed on noticeboards and on 'e-jobs4U'
Rashiv Seduin
(5/10/09)

Figure 11.18 Example verbatim minute

Staffing of NTB clinic

Draft advertisements to be cleared with Personnel and placed on noticeboards and on 'e-jobs4U' **Rashiv Seduin**
(5/10/09)

Figure 11.19 Example action minute

Do not fall into the trap of putting information in minutes because they will be read by those not at the meeting. If outsiders need information to understand the minutes, they should ask the chairperson. Once you start making the minutes full and complete for every reader you will have a small book for each meeting.

They spend ages talking about something and then decide not to do it

In many cases, a group discusses a range of alternatives before deciding on one. Detail on the options that are rejected is not usually put in the minutes, except where there is a clear requirement to demonstrate that the group discussed all options in full and to show the reason for pursuing one policy. This can be done either by detailing each alternative, probably under subheadings, or by grouping them together so they are listed but not developed. Make sure you finish with the alternative that will proceed.

Do I name names?

Minutes that identify who said what are called 'attributive'. Names, initials or job titles can be used, anything which identifies the speaker. Attributive minutes are very wordy and dull to read, and leave the minute-taker open to comments like 'I didn't say that.'

A further problem is deciding who to attribute to. One person may have said it, but several agreed – who got in first is a matter of chance (or the loudest voice). This means that it is often the same few people who make the points and this style means that it seems as though only those few attended.

Attributive minutes also emphasise the differences between group members and can often feed argument rather than report on discussion. Writing attributive minutes will leave the minute-

taker with little choice but to follow the route of the discussion, which is likely to be long and winding. An example of attributive minutes is shown in Figure 11.20.

Staffing of NTB clinic

Sally Munro raised the issue of staffing for the new clinic and suggested a minimum of three nurses would be required for each session. Belinda Parker suggested that a full-time secretary/receptionist would also be needed.

Sally Munro suggested that in order to be as 'family friendly' as possible, the nursing posts should be flexible. Rashiv Seduin disagreed on the basis of the continuity of nurse/patient relationship.

Desmond Isling felt that as the clinic times would fall within normal working hours the administrative post could be one full-time person. Sally Munro suggested this was not necessary and a 25-hour week would cover the workload. She added that there would also not be a problem with holiday/sickness cover as this could be arranged through the other health centre staff. Desmond explained the level of workload and it was agreed that a full-time post was required.

She proposed three 30-hour/week posts or as many part-timers as could cover the shifts. Applicants would have to agree which clinics they wished to cover and commit themselves to those periods. This would mean the same nurse would run a particular clinic each week, leading to continuity for the patients. Belinda Parker asked what would be the position with regard to holiday and sickness periods and it was agreed that part-time staff were preferred as hours could be changed/ increased to provide cover.

> *Draft advertisements to be cleared with Personnel and placed on*
> *noticeboards and on 'e-jobs4U'* **Rashiv Seduin**
> (5/10/09)

Figure 11.20 Example attributive minute (verbatim)

Minutes should be concerned with what was said, not who said it.

What 'person' do I use?

Minutes must always be written in the third person, that is, no reference to 'I', 'we' or 'you', 'your', etc. The common problem is with 'our' and vague references. In the examples in the following box, the reader would not know whether it was the committee, the department, the site or the whole organisation that has problems or concerns.

> **Our problems stem from the introduction of flexitime.**
> **Our concerns centre around the announcement of redundancies.**

Other related problems come with phrases like 'in this area' (which area?) or 'next year' (calendar, academic or financial?).

How do I avoid an inappropriate tone and words?

Minutes must be written from a neutral position, representing the discussion in terms of what was discussed (rather than the style or manner of discussion). Beware of latching on to words that are said in the meeting and then using them. You are likely to follow the clearest speakers (or those you agree with) and the minutes will almost certainly be biased. Listen for the point of view, or message, and note this in your own words – minuting is a skill involving interpretation, not fast writing. Chapter 8 will help with this.

Useful words for minutes

Although an accurate overview of the discussion should lead the minute-taker to the words that are necessary, there are occasions when it seems that the same word is used over and over again. In many cases this is the result of writing script-style minutes (the 'he said, she said' type), and simply removing the 'he said, she said' will reduce the problem, not to mention making the minutes easier to read:

> Mr Heyford explained that there are problems with the system and it is in danger of crashing at any time.
> *Replace with:* There are problems with the system and it is in danger of crashing at any time.

The following are loosely grouped in no particular order. They cannot be used as synonyms; instead think of what you are trying to say and find the nearest alternative:

discussed/debated/deliberated/considered/examined/analysed
said/stated/reported/established/confirmed/verified/declared
pointed out/explained/suggested/drew attention to/raised/
 informed/understood
were reminded that/recalled/clarified/illustrated/defined/
 demonstrated/emphasised
agreed/concurred
disagreed/disputed/not the case
planned/intended/meant/hoped/proposed
existence of/issue of/reality of/topic of/problem of/question of
benefits of/merits of/advantages of/worth/value of
problems/drawbacks/dangers/uncertainty/disadvantages
chose/opted/selected/picked/named/preferred
potential/possibility/likelihood/prospect/chance/probability
options/alternatives/choice/preference/opportunity
decided/resolved/approved/concluded/determined
worried/concerned/troubled/uneasy/anxious/apprehensive

12

Recording decisons and actions

A significant part of the reason for having minutes is to record the decisions that are taken and to remind the participants of what they agreed to do. If the minutes are to fulfil this purpose, they need to be sent out promptly and with actions clearly shown.

Sometimes, there are areas where individual group members are unsure of what was discussed and rely on the minutes for an explanation. In many cases, people rely on the minutes to remind, if not inform, them of the actions they agreed to!

Noting the outcome of discussions does not sound particularly difficult. However, many groups conclude discussion with phrases like 'Right, we'll go with that' or 'Margot, you can take that forward' and the minute-taker is left unsure of what is going to happen.

It is essential that you leave the meeting knowing exactly what the outcomes, the action points, are – the action triangle.

The action triangle

There are three aspects of an action point (see Figure 12.1):

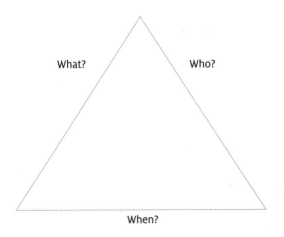

What? Who?

When?

Figure 12.1 The action triangle

- **precisely what is going to be done;**
- **who will take responsibility;**
- **when the action should be completed.**

The 'who' must always be a member of the group. If actions are allocated to someone outside the group, there is no mechanism for feedback. The committee member might do no more than give an instruction to someone, but the responsibility still lies within the group.

An example

Consider this unusually clear summary of a discussion on security given by the chairperson: 'Right, so we're agreed that Reception will not allow anyone in after 5.00 from 2 October. Chris, you'll sort it?' The minute-taker wrote the following:

> Reception not to allow anyone in after 5.00pm. Chris Francis
> 2 October 2009

This is not quite accurate as Reception's system needs to change from 2 October (not the deadline for Chris to take the action) and there is no overt link between Chris and Reception.

When clarifying the action in your mind, it is best to start with 'who?'

answer: Chris

Then ask what is he/she doing?

answer: telling Reception not to allow anyone in after 5.00 from 3 October

Finally, when is that person doing that action?

answer: we don't know, no one said how much notice they would need

The minute-taker should have interrupted to ask, 'When will that need to be done by?' Or, 'How much notice will they need?' It is possible to ask Chris, 'When will you do that?' However, in reality this sounds too much like taking over the job of the chairperson. Once the minute-taker knows the date, the action becomes:

> Reception to be told not to allow anyone in after 5.00 from 2 October.
> Chris Francis
> 21 September 2005

If you are not sure of any aspect of the action (or side of the triangle), you must ask. Interrupt with questions like:

- **'Please could you confirm the action for the minutes?'**
- **'Could you give me a precise action for the minutes?'**
- **'Please could you define the action for the minutes?'**
- **'Who is responsible for that?'**
- **'Whose action is that?'**

- 'What is the deadline?'
- 'When is that to be completed?'

In fact these are some of the easiest interruptions to make because they are so factual. When you interrupt to ask, you will often find that others don't know either.

When there is no outcome

Each minute should be 'closed', that is, a confirmation of how the discussion ended. This is usually an action point, but often there is nothing more to be done or the group did not or could not reach agreement.

If the group agreed there was no need for them to take any action, replace the action with 'No action necessary', following the layout of action points. Although it may be obvious now, this will make the minutes clearer for future readers. This will usually follow items for discussion only (although sometimes these will result in an action).

If the group did not get as far as taking an action (when one was required), the term is 'No decision taken'. You will probably need to ask the chairperson whether to put it on the agenda for a future meeting.

If the group were arguing and could not reach a decision, use 'No consensus reached'. Again, ask whether to include the item on the next agenda.

If it was agreed to discuss the item at a future meeting, the phrasing is 'Deferred to next meeting' or 'Deferred to meeting on [date]'. If the item had to be passed to another group, the action point should be replaced with 'Referred to...'. This latter alternative is likely also to have a reason, for example 'Referred to Health and Safety Committee for advice' or 'Referred to Board for approval'.

Layout of action points

Most people do not read minutes in any great depth. Their concern is to see what was talked about (the heading) and what, if anything, will be done about it (the action). These readers are likely to miss actions that are buried within a paragraph, so the action must be a separate paragraph, even if it is just a few words.

In terms of the layout, there are many ways of presenting an action in minutes. The clearest is an action column, but anything that achieves the aim of clear presentation is acceptable. All the variations in Figure 12.2 would be a separate paragraph and usually indented from the left margin. The first is clearest, followed by the final version. See Figure 13.3 for instructions on creating an action column. Avoid typing the action point in bold as it is likely to be followed by a heading, also in bold, and the action will be visually tied to the wrong heading. The text can be in italics or in a contrasting font.

When there are several actions for one minute

Where possible the minute should be split with subheadings and the resulting action in the appropriate place. This is not always possible, usually because the actions are so interwoven that they cannot be split, but different people may take on aspects of the action. Where this happens, show each aspect of the action separately with the name and deadline. Example layouts are shown as Figure 12.3.

The team decided that the Christmas party would be
open to all staff and their partners. There would be no
charge for staff members but partners would be asked
to contribute £18 to cover food and wine at the table. **Sue Taylor**
Details to be included in November e-news 14 November
 2009

The team decided that the Christmas party would be open to all staff
and their partners. There would be no charge for staff members but
partners would be asked to contribute £18 to cover food and wine at
the table.
Details to be included in November e-news
Sue Taylor *(14 November 2009)*

The team decided that the Christmas party would be open to all staff
and their partners. There would be no charge for staff members but
partners would be asked to contribute £18 to cover food and wine at
the table.
Sue Taylor *to submit details for inclusion in November e-news*
(14 November 2009)

The team decided that the Christmas party would be open to all staff
and their partners. There would be no charge for staff members but
partners would be asked to contribute £18 to cover food and wine at
the table.
ACTION: Details to be included in November e-news
 Sue Taylor *(14 November 2009)*

The team decided that the Christmas party would be open to all staff
and their partners. There would be no charge for staff members but
partners would be asked to contribute £18 to cover food and wine at
the table.
Details to be included in November e-news ***Sue Taylor***
 14 November
 2009

Figure 12.2 Example layouts for action points

The team decided that the Christmas party would be held at The Rainbow and be open to all staff and their partners. There would be no charge for staff members but partners would be asked to contribute £18 to cover food and wine at the table.

Provisional booking to be made at The Rainbow for 120 people	**Ami Chi** 23 October 2009
Details to be included in November e-news	**Sue Taylor** 14 November 2009

The team decided that the Christmas party would be held at The Rainbow and be open to all staff and their partners. There would be no charge for staff members but partners would be asked to contribute £18 to cover food and wine at the table.

Provisional booking to be made at The Rainbow for 120 people
***Ami Chi** (23 October 2009)*
Details to be included in November e-news
***Sue Taylor** (14 November 2009)*

The team decided that the Christmas party would be held at The Rainbow and be open to all staff and their partners. There would be no charge for staff members but partners would be asked to contribute £18 to cover food and wine at the table.

***Ami Chi** to make provisional booking at The Rainbow for 120 people (23 October 2009)*
***Sue Taylor** to submit details for inclusion in November e-news (14 November 2009)*

The team decided that the Christmas party would be held at The Rainbow and be open to all staff and their partners. There would be no charge for staff members but partners would be asked to contribute £18 to cover food and wine at the table.

ACTION: Provisional booking to be made at The Rainbow for 120 people
 ***Ami Chi** (23 October 2009)*
 Details to be included in November e-news
 ***Sue Taylor** (14 November 2009)*

The team decided that the Christmas party would be held at The Rainbow and be open to all staff and their partners. There would be no charge for staff members but partners would be asked to contribute £18 to cover food and wine at the table.

Provisional booking to be made at The Rainbow for 120 people	**Ami Chi** *23 October 2009*
Details to be included in November e-news	**Sue Taylor** *14 November 2009*

Figure 12.3 Example layouts for multiple actions

13

Layout and numbering

Layout

The layout of your minutes is vital. People are generally not that interested in them anyway, so make them look readable and interesting to tempt them to at least skim through. There is also the aspect that people judge the content by the appearance, so if they look a mess, the reader won't trust the content.

The layout for minutes broadly follows the layout for a report but with the important addition of the action points.

Page layout

Minutes can be blocked or indented. Blocked is slightly quicker and easier to type, and may save a few lines (see Figure 13.1).

Indented is the more commonly preferred style because it is easier to read and the layout reinforces the relative importance of the information (see Figure 13.2).

Text can be justified, that is set out with straight left and right margins, but this is often harder to read because of the 'stretching' of the text to meet the margin. Minutes with a 'ragged' right margin are easier to read.

6. **Holiday camps, Summer 2010**
 All the schools that were approached offered the necessary accommodation and facilities but some were priced too highly. It was agreed to proceed with Manor Park School (weeks 1–2), Tolbridge Girls School (weeks 3–5) and Amering Hall (Week 6).
 Confirm bookings with schools above　　　　**David Markess**
 9 October 2009

7. **Family placements**

7.1. Family placement with Mrs Bryant
 Mrs Bryant owns a group of holiday cottages and has offered a cottage for one week, during term time, during April or May 2010 to a family of up to six. It was agreed to ask a volunteer to visit her and, assuming she wishes to proceed, to take up her offer and agree a suitable date.
 Member of voluntary administration team to visit
 Mrs Bryant　　　　**Adam Turner**
 16 October 2009

7.2 The possibility of extending the scheme to family placements was discussed and it was agreed to consider this following the first placement.
 Extending the scheme to be discussed at the
 October 2010 meeting　　　　**Sarah Kaminski**
 21 October 2009

Figure 13.1　Example blocked layout

Using an action column

An action column is the easiest style to read, but few minute-takers use it because of the difficulty caused in typing. It is generally set up in a table in order to get the column but this causes problems in lining up the actions against the text,

particularly if frequent edits are made. There is an easier way that is seldom shown in any manual – see Figure 13.3 for guidance on how to do this in Microsoft® Word.

6. **Holiday camps, Summer 2010**

 All the schools that were approached offered the necessary accommodation and facilities but some were priced too highly. It was agreed to proceed with Manor Park School (weeks 1–2), Tolbridge Girls School (weeks 3–5) and Amering Hall (week 6).
 Confirm bookings with schools above
 Action: **David Markess** 9 October 2009

7. **Family placement**

 7.1 **Family placement with Mrs Bryant**
 Mrs Bryant owns a group of holiday cottages and has offered a cottage for one week, during term-time, during April or May 2010 to a family of up to six. It was agreed to ask a volunteer to visit her and, assuming she wishes to proceed, to take up her offer and agree a suitable date.
 Member of voluntary administration team to visit Mrs Bryant
 Action: **Adam Turner** 16 October 2009

 7.2 The possibility of extending the scheme to family placements was discussed and it was agreed to consider this following the first placement.
 Extending the scheme to be discussed at the October 2010 meeting
 Action: **Sarah Kaminski** 21 October 2009

Figure 13.2 Example indented layout

Headings

The layout of headings should represent their relative importance. So, for example, the heading of item 9 is larger than the heading of item 9.1.

- *Place the cursor where you want the action column to start.*
- At the top of the screen there is a 'ruler' (where you click to insert tabs). To the right of the ruler is a triangle, which marks the right margin. *Click on the right margin triangle and drag it to where you want the action column to be (you can change the placing later if you need to).*
- *Insert tab stops for indents (don't rely on default stops) as required including one just to the right of the right margin triangle* (outside your new margin).
- At the top of the screen there may be an icon for a text box – a square with dotted intersecting lines and an inverted triangle to the right. *Click on the inverted triangle. Choose the option for right border only* (all lines dotted except the right border). If you do not have the text box icon, *select the Format menu, and then Borders and Shading. On the diagram on the right, click on the right margin and OK it.*
- The action column should appear! It is only one line long, so hit the 'Enter' key a few times to give yourself some formatted space.

To use the format:
Type your minutes, using the 'tab' key to move to the tab stop outside the right margin and type the name.

If you need to move the action column:
Highlight the text and drag the right margin icon to a new location. You will also need to move the tab stop to the right of the action column.

Figure 13.3 Simple method for layout of an action column

Assuming 12-point text, headings should be 14-point bold. The most common style for professional-looking minutes is shown as Figure 13.4.

Typing rules

All the usual rules of typing, summarised below, apply to minutes:

<div style="border:1px solid">

5. **Heading 14-point bold**

Text 12-point
 Action, 12-point italic **Name 10-point bold**
 Date 10-point

5.1 **Subheading 13-point bold**
Text 12-point
 Action, 12-point, italic **Name 10-point bold**
 Date 10-point

</div>

Figure 13.4 Example text sizing

One space between words
Two spaces after a full stop, exclamation mark
 or question mark
One blank line between paragraphs
 after a heading
Two blank lines between sections

Layout for 'Present', etc

If you have not numbered 'Apologies' on the agenda, it can be included with the other names in columns at the start of the minutes. If you prefer to number it, leave it as number 1 in the minutes and omit it from the names at the start of the minutes. The arrangement of names in columns can depend on the numbers.

See Chapter 11 for more information on 'Present', 'Apologies', etc.

Numbering

Most minutes are numbered from '1' for each meeting. This is

probably the simplest method, and if reference is made to old minutes it can be done as 4.3/7.09 (item 4.3 of the July 2009 meeting).

Continuous numbering

If items are frequently carried forward, you might want to give an item a number that it will keep throughout its life. This system usually reverts to 'I' for the first item of the first meeting each year. Again, items from a previous year can be referenced as 258/09 (item 258 in 2009).

As the agenda headings and numbering form the basis for the minutes, it is worth giving some thought to the numbering at the early stages of the meeting.

Numbering for subheadings

The simplest system is to use the standard report style, illustrated in Figure 13.5.

If you need to use a fourth level of numbering for an item, this can be done as illustrated in Figure 13.6. If this is necessary for any item in the minutes, it should be done throughout. For example, if item 9 needs a fourth level of numbering, the third level will be '9.1.1'. The third level of all items should then be 'X.1.1' even if there is no fourth level.

6. Heading

6.1 Subheading

(a) **Sub-subheading**

Figure 13.5 Example three-level numbering

6. Heading

6.1 Subheading

6.1.1. Sub-subheading

(a) Sub-sub-subheading

Figure 13.6 Example four-level numbering

Look at the picture

Before you dispatch the minutes, look at them from too far away to read. Do they look professional and invite the reader to read?

14

Impact of the Freedom of Information Act on minutes

Anyone who works in the public sector should be aware of the Freedom of Information Act. This includes NHS trusts and independent practitioners (GPs, pharmacists, dentists and opticians); local and central government, schools and the police. The Act is regulated by the Information Commissioner, who has powers which can result in a fine, or even imprisonment, for non-compliance.

Any member of staff can receive a request for information. Be sure that you know the procedure for dealing with such a request as, in most cases, information must be provided within 20 days.

The Act relates to all documents within the organisation, and in most public bodies. Many of these will be meeting papers. It is not concerned with the style and content of minutes, or of any document. Organisations in the public sector will need to ensure that minutes are written in a way that is appropriate for anyone to read. The concerns fall into three areas:

- **Information can be found. This means that filing systems have to be accurate and easy to use and, on a minor level, that headings are accurate and descriptive.**

- Information is appropriate for disclosure. Unless it can be withheld under the terms of the Act, it may be shown to the public.
- Documents must look professional. Layout, grammar, punctuation and plain English all have a part to play in sending the right message to readers.

Exempt information

There are several exemptions, but the ones most likely to relate to minutes are information that:

- would contravene the Data Protection Act 1998;
- may endanger the safety or physical/mental health of an individual;
- may affect the commercial interests of an organisation or person;
- was given in confidence;
- is intended for publication in the future;
- is available to the applicant by another means.

Impact on meeting papers

All meeting papers are covered by the Act: agenda, briefing papers and minutes. The organisation should have a clear policy that covers all aspects from drafting to destruction.

If there is exempt information in meeting papers, it is only that information that does not need to be disclosed. The remainder of the document must be made available.

Referencing meeting papers

It is essential that you are able to find the information requested.

In order to do this effectively, thought must be given to designing a system that is not only usable by the present staff, but will continue on into the future.

Make sure that all documents carry the name of the group and the date of the meeting.

For most situations it is enough to head the agenda and minutes with the name of the group and date of meeting. Briefing papers should also carry this information, together with the agenda item number.

If you use an alpha/numeric referencing system, it must be on every document. A typical example is:

HSC/2009.3 (Health & Safety Committee/year/month)

Briefing papers would then carry the reference:

HSC/2009.3/6 (Health & Safety Committee/year/month/ agenda item)

A paper-based system

For each meeting, file a copy of the agenda, papers and minutes. You might also wish to indicate information that is confidential and would be excluded from any request. This will save time in checking later on.

If the minutes are changed in Minutes of the previous meeting, it has previously been accepted as good practice to leave the 'master' set of minutes as they stood and attach a note of changes made. This meant that anyone looking at the master set would see that different information had originally been circulated and what was finally agreed. However, it is now important to have the master set correct so that it can be copied easily. If you feel it is important that colleagues can see what was originally circulated for administrative reasons, keep a separate note.

An electronic system

It will be necessary to set up a clear system of folders and sub-folders so that meeting papers can easily be found. This is likely to be in a form such as:

Health & Safety Committee
 2009
 • **October agenda**
 • **October minutes**
 • **October paper 4 (paper for item 4)**

If you wish, you could have a further sub-folder for October and then just the documents of agenda, minutes and papers. A system such as this will mean that you only have to 'search' particular folders for information that is requested.

Health & Safety Committee
 2009
 October
 • **agenda**
 • **minutes**
 • **paper 4 (paper for item 4)**

To keep records in monthly order, number the meeting as well as date it.

Health & Safety Committee
 2009
 • **10 October agenda**
 • **10 October minutes**
 • **10 October paper 4 (paper for item 4)**

Writing minutes

Following the good practice outlined in this book will ensure that minutes can be disclosed, but the essentials are as follows.

Minute what was discussed: summary not script

- Note the points that were made, rather than the words used to make them (see below).

Not appropriate for disclosure	Appropriate for disclosure
It was suggested that asking staff to park in the north car park was a ridiculous idea and there was no chance that people would walk that far when they could park on a side street near the main entrance.	It was suggested that staff would park on the streets near the main entrance rather than walk the long distance from the north car park.

- Listen to the group as a whole and keep your focus on what it discussed, rather than what individuals said. Don't attribute: the group members are unlikely to want their views recorded in a 'he said, she said' style (see below).

Not appropriate for disclosure	Appropriate for disclosure
AB suggested a charge of £2 for up to four hours and £6 for up to 12 hours. CD agreed that long-term parking should be discouraged but pointed out that people would simply pay two lots of £2. EF suggested that a flat rate of £4 a day would be simpler.	The group discussed the amount to be charged for parking …

Group confidential information

- Where possible, group items that cannot be disclosed to make it easier to remove the information at a later date. Remember, a confidential item does not mean the remainder of the minutes cannot be disclosed.

Define action points

- Ensure that the action is shown as being the responsibility of a defined member of the group.
- State precisely what that person is to do.
- Give a clear deadline for the action (see below).

Not appropriate for disclosure	Appropriate for disclosure
The group discussed the location of the temporary offices in the light of problems with car parking. Their use will mean the loss of parking spaces and it was agreed that siting them on the southern boundary would minimise this. Rentablock to be advised in time for delivery and Facilities Department to be asked to cone off the southern boundary. *It was agreed that the Portakabins would be sited along the southern boundary of the public car park.* *Desrene Bibi* *23 October 2009*	The group discussed the loss of parking spaces caused by the use of temporary offices. It was agreed to site the cabins on the southern boundary to minimise this. *Facilities Department to be asked to cone off the southern boundary on evening of 23 October.* *Desrene Bibi* *19 October 2009* *Rentablock to be advised in time for delivery on 23 October.* *Desrene Bibi* *19 October 2009*

- Under 'Matters arising' for the meeting following that deadline, record that the action was completed or, if it was not, give a new deadline so that it can be tracked in the future.

Avoid personal attack

- Again, listen for the point being made, rather than the style.
- Be careful about contentious words (see below).

Not appropriate for disclosure	Appropriate for disclosure
Patients' failure to advise of cancellation was blamed for backlog.	It was suggested that the thebacklog was caused by patients not cancelling appointments they could not attend.

Don't show the mood

- Avoid phrases like 'after heated debate'.

Don't judge

- Your opinion should not come through in the tone of the minutes with phrases like 'the committee eventually decided to...' or 'after lengthy/brief discussion'.

Don't name names unless essential

- Unless unavoidable, don't name people (see below).

Not appropriate for disclosure	Appropriate for disclosure
This was the result of Mary Smith's report.	This was the result of the report into non-attendance at…

Be accurate with your use of English

- It is important to choose words that reflect the views expressed by the group (compare the statements in the box below).

The team agreed that overtime could be paid (it's possible)
The team agreed that overtime should be paid (it ought to happen)
The team agreed that overtime would be paid (it will happen)

Use a businesslike style (unless a particularly informal meeting)

- Avoid slang or jargon.
- Use business terms.
- Don't run words together (eg it's, didn't) (see the following example).

Not appropriate for disclosure	Appropriate for disclosure
The DMT had said it would be OK to use their rest-room providing it wasn't for more than a week.	The Divisional Maintenance Team had agreed that their rest-room could be used for up to a week.

Be accurate with spelling and punctuation and careful with presentation

- Although these do not have a 'freedom of information' impact (apart from clarity), the fact that your minutes may be read by a member of the public or the press means that a professional impression is important.

Useful websites

The Information Commissioner's Office
www.informationcommissioner.gov.uk

NHS website
www.foi.nhs.uk/

Local government
www.lga.gov.uk

Department for Education & Skills
www.dfes.gov.uk/foischeme/

15

Business English for minutes

Most people do not read minutes particularly carefully. Those who were at the meeting 'know it' already; those who were not there are probably not that interested. It is therefore essential that your minutes are clearly written so that even someone who is skimming them will understand the contents.

Clear writing involves well-constructed sentences and paragraphs, use of plain English and punctuation. An added benefit is that well-written minutes reflect well on the minute-taker – a boost to professional pride! The problem is that many minute-takers were not taught the 'mechanics' of writing at school, and this practical aspect of being a minute-taker causes considerable worry.

There are many books on English (plain English, grammar and punctuation), and it is far too large a subject to cover in depth in a book on minutes. However, here are some essentials.

Sentences

- **Keep to a maximum length of 18 words. If you have better things to do than count words, just do a couple of**

sentences and see how many lines they take on your computer (usually about 1.5–1.75 lines). After that it can be a visual check.

- Be aware of what the sentence is about; it should appear in the first few words. Where the subject changes, start a new sentence.
- Change sentence where you change tense/time.

Paragraphs

- Paragraphs should be a maximum of eight lines. Where there is more to say on the subject look for logical breaks according to content rather than just split a long paragraph in the middle.
- The subject of the paragraph must appear in the first line, preferably near the start.
- Try to avoid several one-sentence paragraphs; the reader loses the flow.

Plain English

- Be precise with numbers, quantity and so on (avoid words like few, several, plenty). Use dates rather than 'as soon as possible' or 'sometime next month'.
- Use everyday words that would be understandable to a member of the public.
- Avoid jargon (technical terms, abbreviations, acronyms).
- Write in the positive: what has happened/will happen (rather than what has not). For example, do not write 'The scheme is not suitable for staff aged under 45,' but instead write 'The scheme is suitable for staff aged 45 or over.'
- Avoid wordy phrases (not 'come to a decision to' but 'decided').

Problem punctuation

There are four punctuation items that cause particular problems: apostrophes, capital letters, hyphens and semi-colons. In addition, punctuating bullet points also causes concern.

Apostrophe

- Few apostrophes that join words cause problems, the exception being its/it's. Only use an apostrophe if you can replace it's with it is.
- To place the apostrophe for possession correctly, circle the owner and put the apostrophe on the circle:

Mr Jackson's letter	Mr Jackson's letter
The departments hours	The department's hours
The managers explanation	The manager's explanation
A GPs training	A GP's training
Directors car park	Directors' car park
Secretaries experience	Secretaries' experience
GPs training	GPs' training
Womens refuge	Women's refuge
Childrens toys	Children's toys

Figure 15.1

Capital letter

- **Use capital letters when a full title is given. Just because a word appears in that title doesn't mean it gets a capital when it is used in place of the title.**

The Health and Safety Committee	The committee
Intensive Care Unit	The unit
Dr James Carlton	A doctor must be present
Director of IT	The director attended
The Fraud Prevention Strategy	The strategy

Hyphen

Use a hyphen to join two or three words that need to be 'glued together' to have the meaning you intend.

> An in-depth study
> A half-kilo weight
> Super low floor bus (super, low-floor? super-low floor?)
> No-smoking area
> Walk-in centre

Hyphenate words like co-operate, co-ordinate, re-emphasise, pre-authorise.

Semi-colon

A semi-colon is like a large comma – a bigger pause. If you want to join two simple sentences but need a pause between the two parts, use a semi-colon:

> The sub-committees meet every half term; the full committee meets once a term.

If a list comprises wordy items, one or more might need a comma. In this case use semi-colons to break up the items:

The team are a blend of experience and new ideas: Tom Sargeant was there at the start in 2005; Saleena Ahmed and Rob Dunning joined from other councils in 2007, just before the merger; Mary Swann, Isham Drabez and Rosanna Curtis are graduate entrants this year.

In contrast, a colon is only used to introduce a phrase. (Always use one before a displayed list; only use one when the list is in a sentence if a pause is essential before the list.)

Punctuating with bullets

Bullet points are not punctuation in themselves – they simply guide the reader as to the number of items in the list. They can break up a long sentence or be made up of separate sentences.

If the items in the bulleted list are very short, the only punctuation needed is the introductory colon; only use capital letters if the items are names. If there is more ink in the bullet point than the words, you don't need the 'blob' (although you can put it if you wish).

The concerns raised were:
- cost
- public perception
- security

Once there is more ink in the words, it's probably worth the 'blob', but if the items are under one line in length, and have no other punctuation, the colon is all that is needed.

The concerns raised were the:
- costs that would be incurred
- public perception of the accessibility of the service
- security of the staff

If the items are wordier, they are likely to need some punctuation. The bullets themselves should then have semi-colons with a final full stop.

> The concerns raised were the:
> - costs that would be incurred, particularly at a time where the organisation is looking for economies;
> - public perception of the accessibility of the service;
> - security of the staff (there have been five verbal and two physical assaults in the last six months).

If the text is a series of complete sentences, it should be punctuated accordingly (with capital letters and full stops).

> Three concerns were raised:
> - The plan will incur considerable costs at a time where the organisation is looking for economies.
> - The public's perception of the accessibility of the service may be adversely affected.
> - The security of the staff (there have been five verbal and two physical assaults in the last six months).

16

Building confidence

In most cases, the minute-taker is the lowest member of the hierarchy present in the room. If the group are professional in attitude and recognise the importance of the role, this presents no problem. Sadly, there are many groups that are patronising, demand copying or coffee in the middle of the meeting or simply ignore the minute-taker.

Sometimes though, it is the minute-taker's lack of confidence that adds to or causes the problems. It is not easy to be the 'generalist' in a room full of 'specialists', but there are some things you can do to help yourself.

Creating the right impression

Dress

Wear clothes to blend in with the group. This is not necessarily your interview suit. If they wear pin-stripes, a jacket is in order. If they're dressed in sweatshirts, you can dress down.

Of course it is important to be comfortable, to wear something that makes you feel good about yourself and to wear

'layers' so you can shed with dignity if the room temperature rises!

Movement

Most people scuttle when they're nervous, often hiding behind or cuddling their notepad. To give an impression of confidence:

- **Lengthen and slow your stride a little so you walk with a purpose, but not as though you have a bus to catch.**
- **If you are carrying something, don't hide behind it.**
- **Look at people as you pass.**
- **Open a door fully before walking in.**
- **Close the door behind you to give yourself time to decide where to sit.**
- **Place your papers calmly, taking time to arrange them if necessary.**
- **If you are pouring tea or coffee, do so calmly and slowly.**

Voice

Some people's voices rise with nerves, others go quiet and shaky; almost everyone gabbles. Very few think about how they sound until something has gone wrong and then they look back regretfully. Learn to speak clearly through a simple, three-stage approach:

Stage one

- **In private try speaking in a higher voice than usual, taking it as high as you can without squeaking, and then practise speaking lower than usual.**
- **Practise speaking louder than usual, without shouting, and then quieter.**
- **Try speaking faster than usual (think what you're going to say and then say it very fast), then try speaking slower.**

Just spend two or three minutes doing this, getting your voice under your control. It doesn't matter if you feel foolish as long as no one is listening!

Stage two
In a shop or a situation where you are not known, try whichever of the following is relevant:

- **If your voice rises with nerves, drop it just a little as you speak.**
- **If you tend to go quiet/shaky, speak just a little louder.**
- **Almost everyone should practise speaking slower. Say each word clearly and completely before saying the next; it may feel odd, but people understand you first time! Make sure you breathe in before you speak.**

Stage three
In your office or workplace, repeat stage two above. You shouldn't be so extreme that people notice; just moderate your normal speech a little.

By now you should have some confidence that you have control over your voice, so try the technique in more stressful situations. Before you know it you will be able to 'breathe/take control' in any situation, and you'll find you have more presence and influence as a result.

Conversation
Greet people as you see them or as they arrive, using their names if possible. Before you attend the meeting, identify a couple of areas of 'small talk' you can use to start a conversation. Open questions (starting with what, where, when, how and who) will help get people talking.

If the group are talking before the meeting starts, go and join them. You don't have to contribute, but look at the speaker, smile and nod as appropriate.

Eye contact

Look directly at people as you listen or talk to them. During the meeting, watch the speaker when you are not taking notes.

Expression

Make sure you do not frown in concentration or worry. Smile when you catch someone's eye, and develop a calm and interested expression that you can call upon when required (smile with your eyes, not just your mouth – practise in private!).

Seating

As discussed earlier, you should sit next to the chairperson. Apart from the practical benefits this brings, it also emphasises your status as part of the 'management team' of the group.

Get to know everyone

Use opportunities to chat

At the start of the meeting and during any breaks, join the group who are chatting even if you do not contribute. If you meet participants outside the meeting, remember that they are fellow members of the group and chat accordingly.

Remember personal details

Remember who has had a baby, new job, house move and so on. If necessary make a few notes in the address book. It gives you a personal conversation opener and is very impressive to those on the receiving end.

Coping with put-downs

Some put-downs are real; others are imagined. It is easy to assume someone has ignored you when in fact he or she was

engrossed in thought and didn't see you. Always assume the best intention and best behaviour and react accordingly. Often this was the intention, and even if it wasn't your dignity remains intact. A few examples are given below to illustrate this:

- Someone looks at you, and then pointedly at the tray, saying 'Coffee?' The answer is 'Yes, please.'
- You are sent out to copy something, make coffee or perform some task. Clearly hand the minutes to someone, asking him or her to take notes in your absence. The notes may not be much good, but you'll have made the point.
- Greet first, rather than waiting for someone to say hello to you. Use the person's name, and 'Hello' or 'Good morning' rather than 'Hi'.
- If you are passed by when papers are handed out, ask for a copy immediately. Try to prevent this in the first place by looking expectant and reaching out in anticipation of your copy.
- If you ask for help, for example an explanation, and get a response like 'I suppose this is a bit beyond a secretary', smile sweetly and respond politely but firmly (eg 'I wasn't cut out to be an accountant'). You'll usually find the group sides with you and that there are a few smiles of support around the table.

No matter how you feel, never put yourself down or apologise for existing.

Know your place!

In most offices you will find a set-up similar to the one outlined in Figure 16.1.

A very important person, quite possibly with the job title of director, who earns a lot of money and delegates to...

... an important person, possibly a senior manager, who earns a significant amount of money and delegates to...

... a fairly important person, etc...

... and it ends up with the one who takes the role of minute-taker in meetings.

Figure 16.1

In a meeting there is an important person with the role title of chairperson and a whole group of others. Each of those others brings particular knowledge, skill or experience, and none is any more or less important in the context of the meeting. Each one's salary is completely irrelevant. As minute-taker, don't take your salary into the meeting. What you are paid has nothing to do with it – you bring the skill of taking the minutes and you are no less important than anyone else there.

Remember, don't act like the minute-taker you feel; act like the minute-taker you'd like to be!

Creating Success series

The above titles are available from all good bookshops.
For further information on these and other Kogan Page titles, or
to order online, visit the Kogan Page website at
www.koganpage.com